AUSTRALIAN
Tropical
Reef Life

by
Clifford & Dawn Frith

Underwater Photography
by
Roger Steene & Neville Coleman

ee Islands

Published in Australia
by **FRITH & FRITH** Books
'Prionodura', P. O. Box 581,
Malanda, Queensland 4885
Telephone (070) 96 8105
Facsimile (070) 96 8316

National Library of Australia
Card Number ISBN 0 9589942 4 2

First printed 1987
Second printing 1989
Third printing 1992

Other books in this series:

Australian Tropical Birds
Australian Tropical Reptiles and Frogs
Australian Tropical Butterflies
Australian Tropical Orchids
Australia's Cape York Peninsula
Australia's Wet Tropics Rainforest Life

To
Tom Hopwood
in appreciation.

Foreword

Richard Kenchington, Assistant Exceecutive
icer, Great Barrier Reef Marine Park
thority, Townsville

oral reefs are the world's richest tropical marine
ronments. Remote, exotic, beautiful, biologically
rse and highly productive, they are a source of
ination and wonder.

echnology, through such developments as SCUBA
ng, underwater cameras, semi-submersible coral
ing vessels and high speed passenger craft, has made
s more accessible to increasing numbers of people.
nnology has also led to the degradation of many of the
ld's coral reefs through pollution, over-use,
amation and uncontrolled exploitation of resources.

ustralia is richly endowed with coral reefs and is
ng measures to manage and conserve them so that they
continue to be a source of enjoyment and inspiration
resent and future generations. In Western Australia,
Department of Conservation and Land Management is
eloping a system of marine parks to protect reefs of the
olohos Islands and the Ningaloo Section on its north
t coast. On the east coast the Great Barrier Reef has
inscribed on the World Heritage List and is protected
ne world's largest marine park. The Great Barrier Reef
ine Park Authority is responsible for a marine park of
e 350,000 square kilometres containing some 2,900
s.

he Great Barrier Reef Marine Park is managed on the
s of zoning plans which are designed to provide for
ervation and reasonable use. The majority of the Great
ier Reef is zoned for general use which includes a
range of activities from commercial fishing to tourist
lopment but specifically excludes operations for the
very of minerals. Other, more protective, zones which
er more than 450 reefs are more nearly equivalent to
strial national parks. These provide a higher level of

protection for a representative sample of reefs and set
aside areas for appreciation and enjoyment by the public.
The most restrictive categories, Preservation and Scientific
Research Zones, set aside a small number of reefs
undisturbed by man except for the purposes of scientific
research. The zoning plans are developed by a complex
process which involves extensive consultation with reef
users in order to identify and separate conflicting uses and
establish limits for activities which, if uncontrolled, could
lead to degradation of reefs. The controls applied through
the various zones are summarised in the table of allowed
uses of zones of the Cairns Section given below.

Day to day management of the Great Barrier Reef
Marine Park is carried out by the Queensland National
Parks and Wildlife Service which is also responsible for
complementary State Marine Parks covering adjacent
areas under Queensland jurisdiction. More detailed
information on marine parks may be obtained by
contacting the Great Barrier Reef Marine Park Authority
or the Queensland National Parks and Wildlife Service.

The Great Barrier Reef Marine Park Authority and the
Queensland National Parks and Wildlife Service place
major management emphasis upon education and the
provision of interpretive information. By working with
educators and tourist operators through training programs
and development of materials the aim is to enable reef
visitors to enjoy a high quality informative reef experience
and thus to appreciate and support measures for the
conservation of the Great Barrier Reef. A focal point of this
approach is the Great Barrier Reef Aquarium and
Interpretive Centre in Townsville which houses a living
reef ecosystem, a comprehensive interpretive display and
a large range of interpretive materials available to the reef
user.

This book is a welcome addition to the range of available
interpretive materials on coral reefs. Compact yet
comprehensive it provides a valuable introduction to reefs
and to the animals and plants that the visitor is likely to
find there.

Simplified guide to major reef activities by zones (for details see the Zoning Plan available from the Great Barrier Reef Marine Park Authority).	BOATING DIVING	COLLECTING (e.g. shells, coral, aquarium fish)	LINE FISHING	BAIT NETTING	TROLLING for pelagic species	SPEARFISHING (N.B. Not with SCUBA)	POLE & LINE TUNA FISHING	TRAWLING	CRUISE SHIPS	GENERAL SHIPPING
GENERAL USE 'A' ZONE	Yes	Permit	Yes	Yes	Yes	Yes	Permit	Yes	Yes	Yes
GENERAL USE 'B' ZONE	Yes	Permit	Yes	Yes	Yes	Yes	Permit	No	Permit	No
MARINE NATIONAL PARK 'A' ZONE	Yes	No	Yes	Yes	Yes	No	No	No	Permit	No
MARINE NATIONAL PARK BUFFER ZONE	Yes	No	No	No	Yes	No	No	No	Permit	No
MARINE NATIONAL PARK 'B' ZONE	Yes	No	No	No	No	No	No	No	Permit	No
SCIENTIFIC RESEARCH ZONE	No	No	No	No	No	No	No	No	No	No
PRESERVATION ZONE	No	No	No	No	No	No	No	No	No	No

Introduction

The aim of this small book is to provide the casual visitor or underwater naturalist with an introduction to the immense diversity and ecology of the underwater flora and fauna of the Great Barrier Reef, and we have attempted to deal mainly with species most likely to be seen during a brief visit. It is impossible to cover all plant and animal groups comprehensively in this modest book, but we hope the selected examples provide a stimulating introduction to one of the greatest natural wonders on earth and thus enhance the readers experience and appreciation.

Coral reefs occur in shallower warmer waters of the world where sea temperatures range between 18 to 30° centigrade and seasonally do not fluctuate greatly beyond these limits. The majority of coral reefs are found in tropical waters between the tropics of Capricorn and Cancer. Exceptions occur where warm water currents flow out of this area such as along coastal areas of Florida, Japan, the Hawaiian chain, and Australia. The world's southernmost coral reef lies around Lord Howe Island in the northern Tasman Sea.

Along the eastern coast of tropical Queensland lies one of the greatest underwater wilderness areas on earth — the Great Barrier Reef. Covering an area of 350,000 square kilometres the Great Barrier Reef is the largest living reef system on earth. It extends some 2,300 kilometres along the continental shelf, that is the coastal ledge of shallow sea floor that stretches from the mainland to the deeper oceanic waters, from Lady Elliot Island in the south to Anchor and Bramble Cays in the Gulf of Papua. Siltation from the vast Fly River in New Guinea prevents the development of the reef further north.

As early as 1842 the great naturalist Charles Darwin studied the geological origin of reefs and, although some of his theories regarding their evolution are incorrect, his categorization of coral atolls, fringing reefs, and barrier reefs are still in very general terms applicable today. Oceanic coral atolls develop above deeper waters of the Indian and Pacific Oceans, usually atop subsided volcanoes. There are no typical coral atolls in Australia. In the Great Barrier Reef region fringing reefs occur around the continental islands in the Torres Strait and are also found adjacent to the mainland coast north of Cairns. There are innumerable continental islands along this part of the tropical Australian coast which may vary in size from a mere rocky outcrop to a large forested tropical island (see page 4). The geological history of these continental islands is similar to that of the adjacent mainland.

Barrier reefs occur close to continents in the Indian, Pacific and Atlantic oceans. In the early part of the nineteenth century Captain Matthew Flinders applied the word Barrier to the massive Great Barrier Reef but this name is somewhat misleading because it is not a single barrier reef, as Darwin had envisaged, but is composed of some 2,900 individual reefs. Those nearer the outer part of the reef flat are of the barrier reef type described by Darwin but those nearer the shore have varied geologic histories and are called platform reefs.

When we look at the reef what we are in fact seeing i a thin layer of living coral capping millions of years of accumulated limestone. Fossil evidence shows that cora reefs have existed on earth for some 450 million years b that the Great Barrier Reef is a relatively new structure. Millions of years ago Australia was part of the large southern continent of Gondwana. When Gondwana fragmented Australia remained attached to Antarctica f some time before separating from it some 50 million yea ago to move northward toward the tropics. The Great Barrier Reef development commenced approximately 1 million years ago but the majority of it has evolved with the last two million years. The discovery of fossilised inland reefs such as those at Chillagoe, in north eastern Queensland, indicate that during these millenia many major changes in the sea level have occurred.

The hard, or stony, corals are the chief reef builders a they continuously secrete, and build up, limy skeletons. This immense productivity is, however, aided by millio of microscopic symbiotic dinoflagellate algae called zooxanthellae that live within the coral tissues. Accumulation of debris from fragments of dead coral as well as other marine organisms with calcareous skeleto such as small foraminiferans, some algae and of course shells, add further to the bulk of this massive underwate rampart. Boring organisms such as algae, sponges, wor and molluscs speed up coral sand formation, and coralli algae help to bind and consolidate the reef framework together aided by chemical precipitation of carbonates the reef structure.

Coral reefs grow at about the level of a low spring tid down to depths of approximately 40 metres. The best ti to visit the reef is during a good low tide, particularly extreme low spring tides. There are two tidal cycles eve day, high tide being approximately fifty minutes or so la on successive days. Within every twelve hours there is o low and one high tide. The gravitational effects of the su and moon combine fortnightly at the times of new and f moon to produce more extreme low and high tides calle springs; the minimum tides of the intervening period ar known as the neaps. From March to November the sout east trade winds blow constantly over the reef. From December through to February the northern part of the reef, from Cape York Peninsula down to about Innisfail, subjected to the the north-west monsoon and it is at this time of year that rainfall is heaviest and cyclones may occur. Further south, however, winds are variable and often it is calm for several days at a time.

Nothing is more relaxing and memorable than a sunn calm day exploring the bewildering array of colour and diversity of forms on the reef. We hope this book enhan the pleasure gained from your reef experience.

Reefs & Islands

een Island

REEFS AND ISLANDS

Each outer reef, in very general terms, can be divided into zones and each zone supports different coral communities depending upon its position on the reef, for example whether it is subjected to the full force of the waves, exposed for long periods at low water, or is sheltered. These zones include the outer seaward reef slope, the reef front, the outer reef flat, inner reef flat, a sand flat, a lagoon which may be open or enclosed, and a back reef margin and slope.

The outer reef slope may drop gently down into the deeper waters or be very steep, and in some areas may be almost vertical. It may be terraced or dissected by coral-covered spurs and channels. Corals that grow along the reef slope have varied growth forms depending upon their depth and steepness of the slope. In the deeper slope areas, below 30 to 40 metres, the corals are quite thin and encrusting but nearer the surface waters where light is not a limiting factor coral life is rich and diverse in shape.

The reef front is relatively narrow and receives the full force of the ocean swell. The growth forms of the corals in this area mostly belong to the acroporid and pocilliporid familes and are sturdy and stunted to withstand continual pounding by waves. Behind the reef front is the outer reef flat which is usually very sparsely populated. It is mostly encrusted with coralline algae and corals and is sometimes covered by green fleshy algae. These algal pavements, as they are sometimes referred to, may be as wide as 300 metres. The distinction between the outer and inner reef flat is usually quite clear because the sheltered inner reef flat supports an immense range of coral species. Acroporid, pocilliporid, poritid and faviid coral families are well represented here. Sandy cays and wooded islands may develop between the inner and outer reef flats.

The constant action of the prevailing swell and waves on the reef slopes and reef fronts continually batters and erodes the coral colonies in these locations, and shattered pieces of them are transported back to the sheltered part of the reef to form the sand flat and contribute to lagoon sediments. Lagoons are commonly five to ten metres deep and may be devoid of corals altogether or contain large mounds of rocks covered by many species of branching and massive corals. The large, sometimes isolated, coral boulders or patches of many corals seen on the reef or in lagoons are often nicknamed 'bommies''. The back reef margin and slope, on the leeward side of the reef, are well sheltered and support a wealth and diversity of corals.

Torres Strait to Cairns

In the Torres Strait, the northernmost area of the Great Barrier Reef, t outer seaward barrier reefs are small and dissected by many meandering channels to form deltaic reefs, whilst those nearer the shore are a mosaic numerous small dissected reefs. Some of the larger reefs in this area, suc as Warrior Reef, are grass-covered sandy cays. In this area are many continental islands that are inhabited by seafaring islanders.

Raine Island, off the eastern coast of Cape York Peninsula, is the most seaward of all the vegetated coral cays and is an important breeding grou for sea birds and turtles. South of Raine Island down to about Cairns are narrow barrier reefs called ribbon reefs and closer to the shore are the platform reefs. The continental shelf along this section of the coast is qui narrow, no more than 50 kilometres wide, and its waters are relatively shallow being less than 37 metres deep. A long linear chain of ribbon ree separated from each other by narrow passages lie along the most seawar part of the reef called the outer shelf and their reef front drops off steeply into the Queensland Trench, some 2000 metres deep. Ribbon Reefs may as long as 35 kilometres and up to half a kilometre wide and are subjecte to the full force of waves generated by the south-east trades, and because this inaccessibility due to exposure are the least known of all the Great Barrier Reef complex.

Nearer to the mainland along the inner shelf of the reef are oval-shape platform reefs which may be as long as 25 kilometres, such as Magpie, Hedges, and Corbett reefs, and may be capped with shingle or sandy cay Cays are formed when sand, rubble, and other material is accumulated o reef top by the interaction of wind, tidal currents and wave action. Seeds carried by such dispersal agents as wind, flotsam, or sea birds, germinate form vegetation which in turn helps bind the sand mass together — and s a coral cay or island is formed. Within the Howick Group of reefs, offsho north of Cooktown, various stages of cay development can be seen: Mag Reef has a small sandspit that is covered at high water; Coquet Reef has a permanently exposed platform of reef material; and Watson Island is dominated by mangroves. As cays increase in size and become permane exposed at low water mangroves, grass and herbs, and / or shrubs and tre establish themselves. Tracts of large coral boulders, ridges and ramparts coral shingle may accumulate around the cays, particularly on the more exposed windward sides of them.

Low Is

ncourt Reef

haelmas Cay

Vegetated coral cays are particularly common from just north of Cooktown south to about Cairns and some of them are popular tourist locations. Cooktown, Port Douglas, Cairns and the spectacular continental island of Lizard (**page 6, above**) are tourist centres with access facilities for visitors to enjoy the reef. Lizard Island lies approximately 100 kilometres north of Cooktown, and has a research station and one of the most northerly Great Barrier Reef island resorts on it. Some 1,000 hectares in size, with a highest point (Cook's Lookout) of 359 metres, Lizard is an excellent base from which to explore the reef. From here people can visit Cook's Passage, see ribbon reefs along the outer reef shelf, and explore several platform reefs and coral cays as well as enjoying the fringing reefs around the island itself. From Port Douglas high-speed catamarans transport visitors to Low Isles (**opposite**) and nearby Agincourt Reef (**left**) to experience the amazing underwater reef wilderness by snorkelling, by gliding over it in a glass-bottom boat, or from a small underwater observatory. Low Isles, recorded on charts by Captain Cook in 1770, was the base for the first major scientific studies of the Great Barrier Reef in 1928-29. Today its only residents are lighthouse keepers. Low Isles and the more northerly Three Isles (**page ii**) consist of a wooded cay and a mangrove-dominated islet with tracts of coral boulders and shingle ramparts around part of their outer perimeter.

The tropical city of Cairns is a major north Queensland tourist centre and an excellent base from which to visit the reef. Green Island (**page 3**), named by Captain Cook, is a wooded coral cay approximately 27 kilometres offshore from Cairns. Due to its proximity to the mainland it has for many years been the most popular reef attraction. On the island is a resort and an underwater observatory. Today, however, with many high-speed catamarans operating out of Cairns it is possible to reach some of the more remote areas of the Great Barrier Reef; such as Hastings, Arlington, Flynn, Milln, Thetford, Moore and Sudbury Reefs. Facilities are now available for visitors to stay longer than a day actually on the reef. Anchored offshore of Michaelmas Cay (**left**) is a small floating catamaran hotel that caters for day visitors and for over-nighters. Snorkelling and scuba diving facilities and a semi-submersible viewing vessel allow visitors of all ages to enjoy the immense diversity and bewildering array of reef colour and form. Michaelmas Cay not only has good reefs around it but is home to large numbers of breeding seabirds.

Michaelmas Cay is a National Park and it is most important that visitors remain on the beach and do not walk inland into the sea bird colonies. Eggs laid in small sandy depressions are easily trodden on, frightened chicks may stray from their nest and adults are easily disturbed and may break eggs in their fright. This coral cay was one of the first drilling sites selected by the Great Barrier Reef Committee, used to understand something about reef evolution and geological origins.

Lizard Isl

Hayman Isl

on Island

Cairns to Mackay

The continental shelf in this area of the Great Barrier Reef is very wide reaching up to 120 kilometres off the Whitsunday Islands, and lies beneath 40 to 70 metres of water. The seaward shelf drops off into the Coral Sea Platform which is less than 1,000 metres in depth. The reefs are all of the platform type and some are quite large with sandy lagoons and a few such as Beaver Reef and the Barnett Patches have small sandy cays on them that are exposed at low water. Most are some distance offshore but Hardy, Hook, Bait and Black Reefs can be visited from the Whitsundays. Davies and John Brewer Reefs are accessible from the tropical city of Townsville. Townsville has two unique facilities to offer reef visitors. On the John Brewer Reef is an enterprising multi-storey first-class floating hotel that is the first of its kind to be actually located on the reef. In Townsville city itself is an immense walk-through underwater artificial reef observatory and conventional reef aquarium administered by the Great Barrier Reef Marine Park Authority as a major tourist and educational facility.

Along this part of the Queensland coast are some of the world's most spectacular and picturesque tropical continental islands. These include, south of Cairns; Fitzroy, Dunk and Bedarra of the Family Group, Hinchinbrook, Orpheus, Magnetic; and South Molle, Hayman (**opposite below**), Hamilton, Daydream, Brampton, Long and Lindeman of the Whitsunday Group and on each of these there is at least one first-class tourist resort. Around most of these islands are magnificent fringing reefs.

kyn Islands

Mackay to Lady Elliot Island

The shelf in this area is even wider than the Cairns to Mackay area reaching up to 300 kilometres, and the waters are extremely deep at 60 to 130 metres. Its reefs, of the platform type, may be sandy or shingle cays with or without vegetation. There are two major groups of reefs in this area. The remote, very beautiful, and often large (some are over 100 square kilometres in area) reefs of the Pompey Complex and Swain Group lie over 150 kilometres offshore and are separated from the mainland by the very deep Capricorn Channel.

The second group of reefs, the Capricorn-Bunker Group, lie some 80 kilometres off the coast of Gladstone and because of their relative proximity to the coast are popular tourist locations. Forming the Capricornia Section of the Great Barrier Reef Marine Park, they cover an area of 12,000 square kilometres and consist of 34 reefs of which 13 are coral islands. Lady Elliot, just south of the Tropic of Capricorn, is the southernmost in this group and marks the beginning of the Great Barrier Reef. Heron Island (**above**) with its tourist resort, *Pisonia* tree woodlands, and the adjacent and very picturesque Wistari Reef, is the focal point for most tourist activities in this area. Research stations on Heron and One Tree islands provide scientists with facilities to study the complex and intricate reef ecosytems and associated marine life. These island are important breeding grounds for sea turtles and sea birds. The picturesque cays of Hoskyn Islands (**left**) are unusual inasmuch as the eastern one is a shingle cay and the western a sandy one.

REEF PLANTS

Some 12 species of sea grasses and 500 kinds of green, red, brown and blue-green algae occur in the Great Barrier Reef region. Reef plants are essential members of the reef community for they provide food for the herbivorous animals, and offer protective shelter for many reef animals. They also play a part in reef-building and consolidation.

Reef plants are the primary producers of food in the sea and form the basis of the reef's complex and intricate food web. Like most plants they manufacture food by a chemical process called photosynthesis. This is the process by which the sun's energy is used to convert carbon-dioxide and water into food for the plant's growth, of which oxygen is a waste product. Large fleshy reef plants are eaten by herbivorous snails, sea slugs, fish, turtles and dugongs. Microscopic floating plants such as diatom and dinoflagellate alage, known as phytoplankton, provide food for minute free-swimming animals such as crustaceans, coelenterates and an innumerable variety of larvae, all referred to as zooplankton. Other minute dinoflagellate algae called zooxanthellae live symbiotically within the tissues of corals and indirectly play an essential reef-building role. The energy-rich food the algae manufacture during photosynthesis not only feeds them but also provides a large amount of food for its coral host (see page 10). In return the zooxanthellae use some of the corals' waste products for their own nourishment. Clams too have a symbiotic relationship with zooxanthellae, as do sponges and ascidians with minute blue-green algae.

Encrusting calcareous red coralline algae, the lithothamnia (**above**), spread out over the surface of the reef cementing and consolidating the whole reef framework together and in so doing increase the reef's resistence to wave erosion. Pavements of coralline algae often occur on the outer reef flat which is very exposed and continuously subjected to hammering by the waves.

Other algae, such as the seaweeds, may be club-shaped, branched, filamentous, feathery or disc-like and many, particularly Turtle-weed *Chlorodesmis fastigiata* (**page 33, below**), play host to numerous reef-dwelling animals. The green Sea Grape *Caulerpa racemosa* (**above**), is one of the most conspicuous green algae on the reef and exhibits many growth forms. Some green algae have lime-encrusted tissues, such as species of *Halimeda* (**right**) and are, therefore, important reef-builders. When they die segments of their branches , along with other dead calcareous algae, coral fragments, and shells, contribute greatly to coral rubble, sand and lagoon sediment. The boring action of some blue-green algae further aids breakdown of dead skeletons. They also attack live corals and damage and destroy parts of coral colonies, but the dead fragments do contribute to the building up of the reef.

Each year long streaks of rusty red surface water may be seen about the the Great Barrier Reef. Called a red tide, this strange phenomenon is found in tropical waters throughout the world and is the result of a reproductive bloom of countless millions of blue-green algae called *Trichodesmium*.

Coelenterates

COELENTERATES

Without coelenterates there would be no reef, for this group includes all of the corals, besides such well-known creatures as jellyfish and sea anemones. The three classes of animals called Scyphozoa (jellyfish), Hydrozoa (hydroids, hydrocorallines, siphonophores) and Anthozoa (hard corals, black corals, sea anemones, soft corals, blue corals, sea fans, sea whips and sea pens) belong to the coelenterate group. These animals possess stinging cells on the tentacles that surround the "mouth". The stinging cells are concerned with feeding and defence. The body of these animals takes on one of two forms. It is either a cylindrical-shaped sedentary polyp with a flattish base and a mouth at the top surrounded by the tentacles, such as a sea anemone or a colony of corals; or it is a mobile umbrella-shaped individual called a medusa with a mouth surrounded by tentacles that hang down in the water, such as a jellyfish.

Hard corals

There are some 300 to 400 species of hard, or stony, corals on the Great Barrier Reef, some occurring in shallow waters and adapted to exposure at low water and others dwelling in deeper waters. There is an extraordinary variety of shapes and patterns and colours. Differences in skeleton structure, polyp size and shape, and the way in which a colony is formed are the principal basis on which the classification of hard corals is based.

The coral reef is indeed an awe-inspiring place to visit and it is hard to imagine that its massive structure is built by millions and millions of coral polyps that may be no more than one centimetre in diameter. The reef-building hard corals obtain the food necessary to manufacture reef skeleton either by catching it themsleves or by utilising symbiotic algae to do it for them. Corals are carnivores and expand their polyps and tentacles to feed mostly at night. When the tentacles come into contact with suitable planktonic prey stinging cells release barbed threads to sting and immobilise the victim. The graceful tentacles then bend toward the mouth to pass food into it. Digestion takes place in the "stomach" of the polyp and nutrients are then available to the whole colony because the polyps are joined together by lateral extensions of their body walls and as a result are in constant beneficial communication.

Within the tissues of the reef-building hard corals are billions of small algae called zooxanthellae. The algae carry out photosynthesis, the process by which most plants produce food using the sun's energy (see page 8). About 95% of the food the zooxanthellae manufacture leaks out into the coral tissues and is then available to the coral polyp for its growth. During the day these corals feed from their symbiotic algae, and at night they feed themselves!

Corals that support symbiotic algae must live in shallow waters, generally in depths less than 30 to 40 metres, because their plant partners require light to manufacture food. Interestingly, coral species that

10

live in deeper and dimmer waters have the greatest proportion of photosynthesising surface with a relatively tiny proportion covered by the plankton-catching polyps. This clearly emphasises just how essential it is to maximise the amount of light reaching the symbionts so that they can supply the coral with food that is not only essential for the growth of the colony itself but also for the building of the whole reef structure. Corals that do not utilise algae grow in darker and deeper areas of the reef because light is no longer necessary to them, and many even survive in areas of complete darkness.

For only a few nights each year, during a full moon in late spring or early summer, one of the most incredible of natural phenomena can be witnessed on the reef. Each coral polyp may be a male or female or may be hermaphroditic, which is to say it may produce both eggs and sperms. Just prior to spawning the eggs, sperms, or egg-sperm bundles (**opposite above**) collect just below the mouth of the polyp. After dusk when the moon and sea temperature are suitable many different species of corals such as staghorn corals simultaneously release vast numbers of eggs and sperms into the sea (**opposite below**). It has been suggested that an over-abundance of reproductive cells in the water "swamps" predators with so much food that at least a significant percentage of cells will remain to ensure survival of the coral species and the reef as a whole.

A fertilised egg develops into a larva called a planula and it is the free-living planula that settles onto a suitable substrate and develops into a coral polyp. In some coral species the eggs are fertilised within the polyp and it is the planulae that are shed directly into water. As the tiny cup-like young polyp grows it starts to secrete a limy skeleton around itself. It will either remain solitary or, as is more typical, buds off hundreds of identical polyps to form the new coral colony.

The structure of a coral polyp is clearly illustrated in the photograph of the faviid coral, *Favia favus* (**above**). Each coral polyp consists of two layers of cells that surround a central cavity, or coelenteron, with an upper opening or "mouth" surrounded by six, or multiples of six, tentacles. Each coral polyp secretes around itself a cup-shaped exoskeleton of calcium carbonate (limestone) called a corallite. The outer tubular wall of each corallite is called the theca and radiating inwards from the base of it are vertical partitions called septa. The septa may fuse below the polyp to form a central rod or columella. The secretion of calcium carbonate is continuous and as the corallite grows the polyp is pushed outwards so that it remains on the surface of the coral skeleton , or corallum. In some other faviid corals the individual polyps and their patterns are less recognisable as their corallites merge into one another and are indistinguishable. These are the brain corals such as *Platygyra sinensis* (**opposite above**) and *Platygyra lamellina* (**left**), some colonies of which may reach two metres in diameter. The corallites lack internal walls and are arranged in series to form a pattern of wavy ridges and valleys of maze-like intricacy. Similar in appearance to these brain corals are members of the mussid family of corals. The agaraciid corals also have similar patterns of ridges and valleys but instead of being brain-shaped are arranged concentrically on large plates. Colonies of faviid, mussid and agariciid corals occur on reef flats and reef slopes.

11

The family of corals called the acroporids is one of the most diverse and abundant groups of hard corals on the reef. They are the dominant corals of reef slopes and reef fronts and are particularly common within the shallower waters of reef and sand flats. Even a small patch of reef may have hundreds of acroporid colonies growing on it of various shape, sizes, and colours. It has been estimated that they cover about eighty percent of the reef's surface. Colonies show immense variation in form, and a single species may exhibit quite different growth patterns as a result of different environmental conditions. Some are encrusting or leaf-like whilst others are plate-like, bushy, or staghorn shaped (**see page 9, 10 below, and right**). Staghorn coral polyps may be coloured yellow, brown, pink, blue or a vivid purple as in *Acropora secale* (**opposite above**). The branching growth form is typical of many corals but is best illustrated within the staghorn family. Branches increase the surface area of a coral colony, thus ensuring polyps receive maximum exposure to the plankton in water currents and sunlight for their symbiotic algae to be able to feed. Growth rates of coral species vary and growth within a single species will differ according to water temperature, available food supplies, and position on the coral reef. Acroporid corals grow very much faster than most corals and colonies can grow as much as twenty centimetres a year.

Walking over the exposed reef at low water is a most pleasant and instructive experience (**right**). It must be remembered, however, that even one person walking over the reef can cause much damage, particularly to the branched and delicate coral forms. Whilst reef-walking may be the only way some people are able to enjoy the Great Barrier Reef it must be realised that walking on the reef is extremely damaging to it; and that many years of growth can be destroyed by each step of each person. The daily tread of hundreds of tourists will quickly kill large reef areas, which in turn makes countless thousands of associated animals homeless. Thus, when walking on the reef every effort must be made to tread only on flat sandy or rocky areas.

Branching staghorn-like growth forms are also exhibited by members of the pocilloporid family of corals, and branch tips of some species may be needle-like. These corals, such as *Pocillipora verrucosa* (**opposite below**), are easily recognisable by wart-like growths that cover their surface. Species of pocilloporid corals show marked changes in growth form according to environmental conditions. In deeper waters the branches are quite thin and open but in areas exposed to heavy wave action the branches become sturdy and stouter.

Corals play host to many reef-dwelling animals. The Coral Blenny, *Exallias brevis* (**opposite below**) seeks refuge on or between *Pocillopora* coral and is so well camouflaged to match it that it is difficult to distinguish from the coral on which it lives. The coral gall crab, *Hapalocarcinus marsupialis*, is another resident in pocilloporid corals where it lives within small hollows on the branches. Its larvae settle on the coral surface causing the coral skeleton to grow around it. Eventually a small protective chamber is formed in which the adult crabs reside. The female is much larger than the male and she becomes entombed within her gall for life. She spends her time laying broods of larvae within her coral cage. The male can squeeze in and out of the small opening of the cage and visits her to mate!

Within the dendrophyllid coral family there are, as the name suggests, branched tree-like species; but others exhibit a variety of shapes, even within the same genus. Some species of dendrophyllid corals called *Turbinaria* are amongst the most variable of all hard corals to the extent that it is often difficult to identify a shallow growth form and a deep growth form as members of the same species. Colonies may be vase-shaped as in the large *Turbinaria frondens* (**opposite**) or spatulate as in *Turbinaria peltata* (**left**). They occur in a wide variety of situations on the reef and may form colonies of several meters in diameter. The skeletal cups or corallites of *Turbinaria* corals are well separated from each other so that each coral polyp is quite distinct (**left**). These polyps occupy a relatively small area of the total surface of the colony and perform the task of capturing food particles from the sea. The remaining larger surface area is covered by a thin layer of coral tissue that contains the all-important symbiotic zooxanthellae. This larger surface area allows the millions of algae to carry out photosynthesis (see page 10) to produce food, a large proportion of which is shared by the coral.

Some members of the dendrophyllid coral family do not possess symbiotic algae at all and have to rely entirely on their own coral polyps to capture all of their nutrient supply. They grow more slowly than their relatives with algae, and most of them are not large and are certainly not considered to be important reef-builders. One such coral is the small and delicate golden Daisy or Sunshine Coral, *Tubastraea aurea* (**below**). It lives in dark places such as overhangs, crevices and caves. Its tubular corallites grow in clusters from a common skeletal base. Although their polyps normally expand at night to feed on zooplankton it is not unusual to see them open in shadier situations during the day. This beautiful coral is eaten by the Wentletrap Snail, *Epitonium imperialis*, and the beautiful nudibranch mollusc *Phestilla melanobrachia*. The Wentletrap snail eats out much of the polyps and then lays strings of bright yellow eggs in each of the eaten out corallites. The nudibranch, however, eats all the living tissue leaving only white skeleton in its wake.

The small unattached button coral called *Heteropsammia cochlea* is also a member of the dendrophyllid family. A button coral may be solitary or form a colony of a few individuals. It lives on sandy substrates and although it is seldom seen we mention it here because of its very strange life-style. The coral appears extremely mobile but this mobility results from a very unusual association with the peanut worm *Aspidosiphon corallicola*. Initially, a coral larva settles on a dead snail shell and as it grows slowly engulfs the shell. Before the shell is completely engulfed, however, a peanut worm takes up residence and maintains a tunnel through the coral from its shell-home to the outside! The worm moves around in a series of jerky movements swallowing sand from which it extracts its own food and at the same time carries the coral about with it and in so doing keeps the coral stable and upright so that it remains free of sediment. In return the coral provides a comfortable and protective home for the peanut worm.

The mushroom corals are some of the most widespread and abundant corals of sandier reef substrates, particularly in small pools and lagoons. They belong to the fungiid family of corals that, unlike most other corals, are not attached to the substrate. Some members of this family are colonial but mushroom corals such as *Fungia fungites* (**right**) consists of one very large solitary coral polyp with a disc-shaped skeleton or corallite that may reach up to 15 cm in diameter. Numerous limy partitions radiate from the edge of the disc inwards. The dent in the centre is the position of the polyp's mouth and from which the tentacles that bear the food-capturing stinging cells extend when the coral is feeding. Mushroom corals are so-named because they resemble overturned mushrooms without their stalk. When they are young they are in fact attached to a stalk but as they grow they break off it. Mushroom corals favour the more sheltered areas of the reef because they are unattached and are therefore subject to disruption in exposed waters.

Corals belonging to the poritid family often form large colonies and the skeleton is quite porous. Unlike the large single coral polyp of the mushroom corals, those of poritids are extremely small so that the outer surface of the colony appears solid and very smooth. The growth of poritids is remarkably slow and a colony may grow as little as one centimetre a year. In deeper waters some species of *Porites* become mound-shaped, and very old colonies may reach 10 metres across and contain over a 100 cubic metres of limestone rock! Other poritids such as *Porites nigrescens* (**see page 20**) form massive coral gardens of branched colonies.

On shallower reef flats, particularly in sandy lagoons, flattened structures called micro-atolls develop. As their name implies, these are rings of living coral of a colony that has grown into the shape of a miniature "atoll". Several coral species may adopt this growth form but it is most commonly seen in poritid corals such as *Porites lutea* (**right**). Micro-atolls develop as a result of the influence of low tides. A poritid colony grows out radially and upward but when it reaches low tide level its surface dies due to continual exposure to the air and sun, and the rest of the colony continues to grow out horizontally to form the micro-atoll shape seen here. A micro-atoll may grow to several metres across, and several may develop side by side in shallow sandy lagoons. Often the centre of the micro-atoll dies altogether, becomes hollow, and is colonised by corals and other reef-dwelling animals. Corals do in fact play host to many reef animals, such as the beautiful Christmas-tree Worm (**see page 28**), without being significantly harmed by their tenants.

The polyps of some poritid corals such as the *Goniopora* species are unusual because they remain expanded at all times except when touched. It is very easy to recognise these "daylight" corals on the reef for their polyps, capped with tiny tentacles, are exceptionally long and reach about ten centimetres or more in length. Colonies of *Porites* and *Goniopora* are male or female and in most species the sperms released from male colonies swim directly to female colonies and fertilise the eggs internally. This is unusual, because most corals release their eggs and sperms directly into the water where fertilisation is external.

Sea anemones and relatives

Sea anemones, tube-anemones, bead and pavement corals are closely related to the hard corals and black corals but differ from them in that they lack a skeleton. On the reef there are many species of sea anemones and they occupy a great variety of microhabitats. Some even hitch rides on snail shells that are inhabited by hermit crabs! Each anemone consists of a single polyp that like a coral polyp, has six or multiples of six tentacles laden with stinging cells around its mouth. Sea anemones attach to a substrate by a basal sucker-like disc. A few anemones such as the rather drab Fire Anemone *Actinodendron plumosum* will inflict a severe sting if touched. Sea anemones may be very small or like the Giant Sea Anemone, *Stoichactis kenti* (**page 17**), may reach up to one metre in diamater. The tentacles of many species of sea anemone, including the Giant Sea Anemone, are home for the beautiful clown anemone fishes such as *Amphiprion perideraion* (**page 17**), as well as certain shrimp species.

The bead corals or coralliomorphs, the pavement corals or zoanthids, and the tube-anemones or cerianthids, have anemone-like polyps. Bead corals are so called because their club-shaped tentacles resemble, when expanded, a mass of beads. Pavement corals (**right**) are usually colonial and their polyps are linked together by creeping tubes called stolons. Large carpets of pavement coral may cover areas of reef crest or encrust large coral boulders. Tube-anemones or cerianthids (**below**) are a group of sea anemone-like animals that live permanently in sandy mud within a protective tube of mucus which they secrete themselves.

Soft and blue corals

Soft corals, blue corals, sea whips, sea fans and sea pens (see page 20) belong to the same class of coelenterates, called the Anthozoa, as hard corals, black corals and sea anemones, but differ from them because each of their polyps has eight feathery-looking tentacles (not six) around the mouth.

There are many species of soft corals on the Great Barrier Reef, particularly on reef flats. Colonies of soft corals may be delicately branched and brightly coloured as in *Dendronephthya mucronata* (**left**) or lobed and leathery as in *Sarcophyton trocheliophorum* (**below**). Colonies of *Sarcophyton* may be as large as a metre in diameter. Their polyps are all inter-connected and the base of them is embedded within a jelly-like substance called the gelatinous matrix. Each polyp has eight feathery tentacles around its mouth which, when disturbed, can be withdrawn into the soft matrix, so that colonies can change their appearance dramatically. Polyps are often seen expanded during the day, but only when they are covered by water. This is to allow the millions of algae called zooxanthellae they harbour in their tissues to carry out photosynthesis and produce food for themselves and for their soft coral hosts. Soft corals, unlike the hard corals, do not secrete an outer skeleton but have an internal one. This consists of small calcareous spicules or larger rods.

Often bits of red "organ-pipe"- like material are found washed up on the beach. These pieces of coral skeleton belong to the Organ Pipe Coral, *Tubipora musica* of shallower reef waters. Its red skeleton colour persists after death.

The beautiful Blue Coral, *Heliopora caerulea* (**right**), is found mainly in warmer waters of the northern part of the Great Barrier Reef. Blue corals play an important part in some areas as reef-builders because under the right environmental conditions they can produce massive skeleton formations. On reef flats extensive gardens of blue coral, sometimes intermixed with other corals such as the branching poritid coral *Porites nigrescens* (see photograph), may be seen. In life its blue colour is masked by brownish living outer tissue but when dead and dried the skeleton is a vibrant indigo blue.

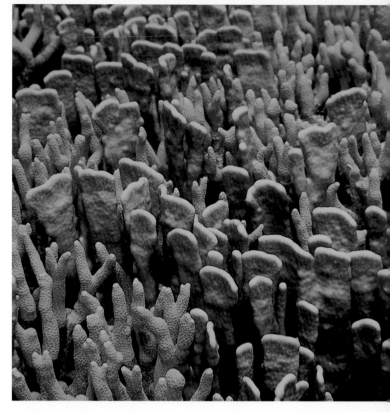

Sea whips, sea fans and sea pens

Sea whips and the bushy or branched colonies of sea fans (**opposite**) are called gorgonians because their skeleton is composed of a flexible but strong horny substance called gorgonin. The skeleton consists of an axial rod from which side branches bearing the live polyps arise. In the sea whips the side branches are minute so that the colony appears whip-like but in the sea fans' side branches are extensive and often inter-connected so that colonies of them appear either bushy or fan-shaped. One end of the skeletal rod firmly anchors the colony to the substrate. Sea whips and sea fans occur mostly in deeper waters along reef slopes and around coral bases, although a few species such as *Rumphella aggregata* (**below**) are quite common in shallower waters. This is because the living tissues of this somewhat less attractive species of gorgonian contain symbiotic algae which need sunlight to manufacture food. The gorgonian benefits from the food produced by the algae, and so it is to the coral's advantage to grow in areas of high light intensity.

Sea pen colonies occur in soft sandy sediments usually in deeper waters and are polymorphic, which means that there are several kinds of polyps, each kind having different jobs to perform. One central polyp is concerned solely with anchoring the whole colony to the substrate whilst those branching from it are concerned with feeding. The polyps are supported by a calcareous axial skeleton. Colonies of sea pens grow at right angles to the prevailing water current so that tentacles of the feeding polyps can efficiently sieve out and trap food.

Very beautiful dried yellow, orange, or red sea fan skeletons are often seen in shell and coral displays, as is shiny black polished jewellery made from the flexible horn-like skeleton of black corals. The whip-like or bushy black corals are more closely related to hard corals than to gorgonians. In life black corals are not in fact black. A thin veneer of living tissues which may be yellow, orange, brown or grey covers their black skeleton. Black corals occur along reef slopes usually in deeper waters and will not be seen during a casual visit, but we mention them here because visitors may see the so-called black coral jewellery for sale in tourist outlets along the tropical coast.

Hydroids and relatives

Another major group of coelenterates is the Hydrozoa which usually have both polyp and medusoid forms in their life cycle (see page 10). The polyp stage usually consists of several polyps joined together to form a branching colony. The polyps within the colony have different tasks to perform, such as feeding or reproduction. This division of labour between the individual polyps is referred to as polymorphism. Reproductive polyps produce jellyfish-like medusae which they release into the water and it is these free-living forms that reproduce sexually, expelling eggs and sperms into the water where fertilisation takes place. Each fertilised egg develops into a small larva called a planula and this reproduces asexually to form the new polyp stage which may be permanently attached to a substrate and lack a skeleton in the case of hydroids, have a calacareous skeleton as do hydrocorallines, or be free-floating and jellyfish-like as are the siphonophores and near relatives.

Hydroid colonies are usually erect and grow attached to coral rubble and debris on the reef flats or from beneath coral overhangs. One of the most conspicuous hydroids to be seen on the reef is the Stinging Hydroid or Fireweed, *Aglaeophenia cupressina* (**right**). This fern-like hydroid attaches to rubble and boulders on the reef flat. If accidentally brushed against it will, as its names suggests, inflict a nasty painful sting and some swelling; but which is not serious. A close relative, the White Stinging Weed, *Lytocarpus philippinus*, also stings but occurs in deeper water and is less likely to be encountered.

Hydrocorallines consist of two groups of hydrozoans called the milleporids and the stylasterids. The yellowish-brown stinging milleporids, sometimes referred to as fire-corals, secrete a massive calcareous skeleton which may reach several square metres. The smaller colonies of stylasterids have a mesh-like appearance and may be blue, mauve or pink. The delicately branched stylasterid called the Elegant Hydrocoralline, *Stylaster elegans* (**right**), lives in sheltered situations attached to the undersurfaces of overhangs or in caverns. The beautiful pink colouration is retained by the dead skeleton. Because of their lacy-look stylasterids are often referred to as lace corals but this name can be confusing as it is also applied to the totally unrelated lacy-looking bryozoans (see page 26).

Siphonophores are free-floating jellyfish-like hydrozoans that have a large balloon-like float. They include the infamous Portugese Man-of-war, *Physalia utriculus*. Hanging from the float are dozens of polyps some of which are specialised for feeding whilst others are concerned only with reproduction. Siphonophores are not likely to be encountered in the reef shallows but we mention them here because they are often found stranded on beaches. They should not be picked up for it is important to remember at all times that these floating colonies can inflict a severe and very painful sting that may endanger the victim's life. Close relatives, the By-the-wind-sailors of the genera *Velella*, have gas-filled bright blue floats and are sometimes encountered in reef waters.

Jellyfish

Another group of coelenterates, called Scyphozoa, are the skeleton-less jellyfish. Jellyfish are creatures of deeper, more open, waters but a few are seasonally seen in shallower reef waters. The umbrella-like part of the jellyfish that varies in shape from a shallow saucer to a deep cup usually lies uppermost in the water with the tentacles and mouth surrounded by lobed "lips" called oral arms hanging down below. Within the "umbrella" circumference are powerful muscles that contract to move the jellyfish up or forward and relax to let it float down, thus propelling the jellyfish in somewhat zig-zag fashion. Jellyfish are predators and feed mainly on small invertebrates which they trap and paralyse using stinging cells on the tentacles and oral arms. The Lions-mane Jellyfish, *Cyanea capillata*, is common in the warmer waters of the northern part of the Great Barrier Reef where it can sometimes be seen in large numbers. The umbrella, or bell, of this large golden-brown jellyfish may reach one metre in diameter and its "mane" of highly elastic stinging tentacles, which may number up to 800 and be ten metres in length, can injure people. Schools of fish such as juvenile trevallies often seek shelter within the jellyfish mane without apparently being harmed in any way.

Some jellyfish do not have a single mouth but have many that open on the oral-arms. These root-mouthed jellyfish, as they are aptly called, include the Upside-down Jellyfish *Cassiopeia audiomeda* (**above**) and the beautiful jellyfish *Mastigias papua* (**see 24**). The former jellyfish is semi-sedentary and has a peculiar habit of lying upside down on the sea floor. Its frilly oral-arms laden with stinging cells lie uppermost and very efficiently sieve through water for planktonic foods.

The most dangerous of jellyfish is the transparent Box Jellyfish, *Chironex fleckeri* (**left**). Box Jellyfish, also called sea wasps or fire-jellies, inhabit shallower muddier waters close to the mainland coast particularly around creek and river mouths in the more northerly waters of the Queensland coast. Although they are present all year round they are notably abundant during the warmer months of October through to April. The semi-transparent bluish bell of this jellyfish is box-shaped and is usually quite small, being no more than 15 centimetres in diameter. Its fine long tentacles hang from each corner of the "box" and have a multiple transverse bar pattern along their length. When fully extended they may be more than three metres in length but can, remarkably, retract to as small as 5 centimetres!

The sting of the Box Jellyfish can be fatal to people and immediate medical help must be sought. A recent medical breakthrough has shown that vineagar applied immediately to the wound inactivates the stinging cells and reduces the reaction to the sting. Pantyhose can be worn when swimming to greatly reduce the chance of being stung. Box Jellyfish are not known to normally occur around coral or offshore islands so that visitors, while being aware of them, should not be too concerned.

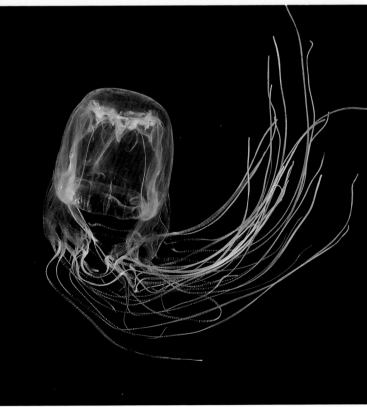

SPONGES, BRYOZOANS and ASCIDIANS

It is hard to realise these inanimate-looking creatures are in fact living animals, as many of them closely resemble plants. Although all of these three groups are quite unrelated we discuss them together here because they are all sedentary and feed by filtering out plankton from sea water. They are found attached to coral, algae, rubble, dead shells, overhangs, crevices and caverns.

Sponges

Sponges belong to the phylum Porifera and are an ancient group of marine animals that have been recorded in fossil records as long ago as 650 million years. Most people think of sponges as something used in the bathroom, without realising that they are scrubbing themselves with the skeleton of an animal. The internal sponge skeleton is made up of spicules of calcium carbonate or silica and / or a fibrous material called spongin. The spicules take on all shapes and sizes and it is these that provide the basis for recognising individual sponge species. The sponge body consists of two layers of cells which may be convoluted to form canals and chambers that give it its "spongy" structure and appearance. Water is drawn into the body cavity through small pores in the body wall called ostia, by the continuous beating of whip-like structures called flagella made of special cells called collar cells or chaonocytes. As the water is pumped through the sponge body food, such as bacteria, is filtered from it and the water, with waste material, exits through a large hole called an osculum.

Sponges range from small to very large and may be encrusting (**see page 46, above**), branched, lobed, tubular, vase-shaped, or cup-shaped as in *Carteriospongia fissurella* (**above**), and are often brightly coloured. Some sponges chemically digest limestone coral skeletons and whilst this boring action is destructive the shattered fragments eventually accumulate as rubble that is necessary for reef building. Such sponges, together with boring worms and molluscs, have been referred to as "destructive builders"!

Many worms, shrimps, crabs and brittle stars live between sponge tissues without causing any harm to the host, and may so gain protection from predators as many sponges produce toxins that are distasteful to many animals. The Sponge Crab, *Dromiopsis edwardsi*, holds a coat of sponge firmly on its back with modified claws on its last two pairs of walking legs, thus cleverly using the sponges' distastefulness to deter predators and avoid being eaten.

Interestingly, these sponge chemical compounds have been examined by pharmaceutical companies as possible antibiotics or anti-cancer drugs, but such research is still in its infancy.

Bryozoans

Minute bryozoans live together in brightly coloured colonies which may be encrusting, branching, or mat-like. Some bryozoans such as *Iodictyum* (**left**) are quite lacy looking and are referred to as "lace corals" but they must not be confused with the hydrocoralline lace corals (see page 22).

25

Some bryozoan colonies are partially calcareous, or hard, whereas others are gelatinous. The individuals within a colony are called zooids and one colony may consist of several thousand of them. The majority of zooids are concerned with feeding, but others can be modified for attachment, support, reproduction or protection. Around the mouth of each feeding individual is a structure called a lophophore which is a cluster of tentacles covered with hair-like cilia that draw food-laden water to the animal's mouth.

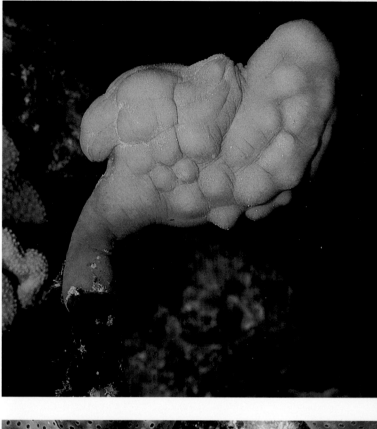

Ascidians

Ascidians, or sea squirts as they are sometimes referred to, are very primitive animals belonging to the phylum Chordata, which also includes fish, frogs, reptiles, birds and mammals. Although they exhibit many features of the chordates they do not have a backbone, as do other members of the phylum. An individual ascidian,or sea squirt, is bag-like and is covered by a jelly-like or leathery outer coat called the test, that is largely composed of a cellulose-like substance called tunicin. The base of the test is thickened to form a hold-fast by which the ascidian is held firmly to a substrate. Often bits of detritus, weeds, or even other sedentary animals become attached to this outer coat and in so doing provide the ascidian with a convenient camouflage. The body has two openings, an incurrent opening through which water and planktonic food is drawn by the action of beating cilia lining the animal's "gut", and an excurrent aperture through which water and waste exits. Many ascidians, and sponges, have a symbiotic relationship with blue-green algae that provides them with an additional food source.

About 200, mostly brightly coloured, ascidians occur in Great Barrier Reef waters living either as single individuals or in colonies. The yellow ascidian called *Polycarpa clavata* (**above**) is a solitary species. It is commonly seen on the reef, attached to the substrate by a thick flexible stalk. Its mouth hangs downwards to avoid catching unwanted sediment and faces into the flow of water, whereas the exhalent siphon throws out waste into the current to avoid contaminating the in-going water current.

Each yellowish-green sac-like structure of the Green Ball Ascidian, *Didemnum molle* (**right, and page 53 below**) is in fact not one single ascidian but a colony of numerous small ascidians. Each individual is called a zooid and the numerous small holes over the surface of the colony are the incurrent openings. Their small excurrent apertures, however, are not visible for they open into the central cavity which itself is open to the sea by the large hole that can be seen at the top of each colony. Star-shaped calacareous spicules are embedded in the test of these colonies to provide them with extra support.

It is hard to recognise the adult ascidian as an animal. Its free-swimming larva is however, more animal-like and resembles a very small tadpole. The larva swims to other areas of the reef and in so doing disperses the ascidian species. Within a few days it selects a suitable shady spot and attaches itself to it by special sucker-like discs on its head. It looses its tail and changes into the sac-like adult. The adults replicate themselves by budding to form an ascidian colony.

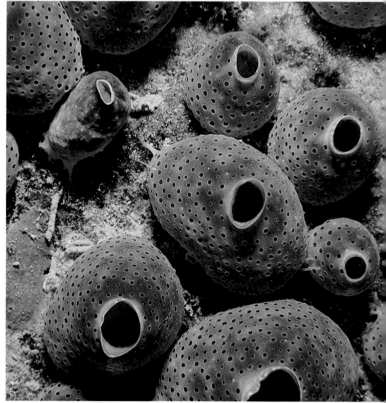

WORMS

Marine worms belong to the six phyla Nematoda, Sipuncula, Echiura, Platyhelminthes, Nemertea and Annelida. The very small hair-like nematodes, the finger-like echiuroid worms, and the tubular peanut worms or sipunculids (see page 15) live mostly amongst debris and coral rubble and are not commonly seen on the reef.

Flatworms

The phylum Platyhelminthes includes many species of colourful flatworms living on the reef, and also includes the not so pleasant terrestrial parasitic liver-flukes and tapeworms. The oval flattened body may be semi-transparent and have frilly margins. Most flatworms are only a few millimetres in length but those on the reef may reach as long as 5 centimetres and, like the beautiful flatworm *Pseudoceros bedfordi* (**left**), may be brightly coloured in a mosaic of patterns. Flatworms live under boulders or amongst coral rubble. Sometimes they are seen gliding over corals, soft sandy substrates or turtle weed. They move over a substrate by firstly secreting a layer of mucus onto it and then, by beating the hair-like cilia on the underside of their body, ride smoothly over it. Some flatworms actually swim through open waters in an undulating fashion, a progression brought about by a series of muscular contractions causing undulations, or peristaltic waves, that ripple continuously down the body length. Flatworms are predatory and capture prey such as small worms or crustaceans with a muscular tubular pharynx that can be rapidly everted through the mouth. Flatworms are hermaphroditic which is to say each individual produces both male and female reproductive cells. They are not self-fertilising but two individuals come together and exchange sperm so that cross-fertilisation is ensured. Most flatworms have remarkable powers of regeneration. If they are broken up into small bits each part will then grow into a new flatworm.

Ribbon worms

Ribbon worms belong to the phylum Nemertea and are so named because of their long, flattened, ribbon-shaped, unsegmented bodies that have remarkable powers of extension and contraction. The five-lined black and white ribbon worm called *Baseodiscus quinquelineatus* (**left**), is a conspicuous species of reef flats where it can be found beneath coral, algae or rubble. Its body can stretch to 30 centimetres or more. Ribbon worms move over a substrate in the same way as flatworms. They are voracious carnivores, feeding upon small worms and crustaceans, and are well equipped to catch their prey. They have a long protrudable structure called a proboscis which in some species is armed with spikes. When not in use, the proboscis is inverted and stored within a cavity in the body but when food is nearby it is everted through a hole above the mouth and its spikes penetrate the victim and a paralysing fluid is injected. Species lacking spikes capture prey by coiling the proboscis tightly around it in a constricting hold.

Polychaetes

Polychaetes are segmented marine worms belonging to the phylum Annelida which also includes earthworms and leeches. Many families of polychaetes occur in reef waters where they occupy many microhabitats. Some are sedentary and live in tubes whilst others are free-living.

The Christmas-tree Worm, *Spirobranchus giganteus* (**below**), is one of the most spectacular and familiar of all the tube-dwelling worms. Colonies of these worms can be found about the periphery of micro-atolls and on other hard corals. Christmas-tree Worms may be blue, green, yellow, red or orange and several colours are often present on one coral colony. Interestingly one individual can produce offspring of different colours. Male and female Christmas-tree Worms release their gametes, that is either sperms or eggs, directly into the sea where fertilisation then takes place. The juvenile worm settles on a suitable coral colony and secretes a small tube around itself. The coral grows around the worm tube and slowly envelops it, save for the opening at the top of the worm tube through which the worm can expand its feathery tentacles. The tentacles of the Christmas-tree Worm are arranged in a double spiral and are divided, or pinnate, giving them a feathery appearance. The tentacles are covered in hair-like cilia. The ciliary beats draw water over the tentacles that very effectively screen off planktonic food. When disturbed the tentacles can be rapidly withdrawn into the safety of the worm's tube.

Long thin creamy-white feeding tentacles are often to be seen extending out from beneath coral debris on the reef. These belong to another tubicolous worm called *Reteterebella queenslandica* that builds a soft tube of mucus to which adhere particles of sand, bits of shell and other detritus. The feeding tentacles convey sediment to the mouth where algae and micro-organisms are extracted from it. At the base of its tentacles are small gill-like filaments that contain the red respiratory pigment haemoglobin — the same pigment that carries oxygen through our own blood.

The free-living, or errant, polychaete worms as they are called, actively move around the reef. They are carnivorous and use jaw-like structures around their mouth to capture small invertebrates. Each of their segments bear a pair of paddle-like structures called parapodia that bear stiff bristles called setae. By muscular contractions passing in waves down the body, in co-ordination with the movement of parapodia and setae, these worms crawl over soft substrates or paddle through the water. Some polychaetes have scales on their backs and are appropriately called scale-worms, and others are bristly and referred to as bristle-worms! Care must be taken not to touch members of the bristle worm family for their bristles are very brittle and easily break off and penetrate into our skin causing an intense burning sensation. Other worms bore into coral skeletons by secreting dissolving chemicals or by grinding their way into them. Thousands of small boring worms may inhabit one dead coral colony, where they gain safety from predators.

Like so many other marine invertebrates the polychaetes liberate their sperms or eggs directly into the sea, fertilisation taking place externally. This habit is associated in many polychaete worms with a phenomenon called swarming. Some polychaetes, when they become sexually mature, undergo bodily changes such as the development of large swimming lobes. In response to a particular environmental cue, perhaps a phase of the moon, swarms of them swim up to the surface waters and synchronously release their eggs or sperms. Other species, such as the Palolo Worm of the reefs of the southern Pacific, break off the posterior part of their body that is laden with eggs or sperms. These body fragments rise in such quantities that the surface of the water writhes with the worms, and is later milky with the discharged eggs and sperms. Palolo worms spawn at almost exactly the same time each year; at dawn on the day of the last quarter of the October-November moon. Many islanders in this area consider the worms a great delicacy and on the spawning day go fishing to catch them from the surface waters.

Crustaceans

CRUSTACEANS

Crustaceans are now placed in a phylum of their own (Crustacea) although for many years they were considered a class of the phylum Arthropoda, which also included insects, ticks, mites, spiders, centipedes and millipedes. There is an immense diversity of crustacean life on the reef. They range in size from minute planktonic organisms to the very large lobsters and crabs. Small crustaceans such as water fleas and copepods and a large number of larvae are the major constituents of zooplankton. Sea lice (isopods), sea fleas (amphipods), barnacles (cirripedes), mantis shrimps (stomatopods), and an immense range of shrimps, crayfish, lobsters, squat-lobsters, crabs, and hermit-crabs (decapods) are all familiar reef-animals; many of which are not only very important in the rich reef ecosystem but are of great economic importance to people. Visitors to Queensland sea food restaurants will quickly become familiar with large and ornate painted crays or reef lobsters, *Panulirus ornatus* and *Panulirus versicolor* (**page 29**).

Crustaceans have a segmented body which is divided into the head, thorax and abdomen. Each segment may bear jointed appendages or limbs that can be specialised for walking, grasping, feeling, digging, swimming, carrying, cutting or feeding. A tough protective yet flexible outer coat or cuticle, largely composed of chitin, covers the body. In some crustaceans this exoskeleton is folded to form an extra covering called a carapace such as crabs have. As crustaceans grow they periodically cast off, or moult, their old skeleton; the new soft body and skeleton then rapidly expands before the new skeleton hardens. The head bears eyes, a pair of long feelers or antennae, a pair of jaws or mandibles, and two pairs of accessory jaws called maxillae.

Many crustaceans are not always easy to see on the reef as most are nocturnal. During the day they remain hidden away amongst algae, coral, sponges, coral rubble, boulders and debris. Some crustaceans are carnivorous, some herbivorous, and others obtain their nutrients from bits of organic detritus and are therefore referred to as detritivors.

In the majority of crustaceans the sexes are separate and the male transfers the sperms, often in a small packet, directly to the female. Typically the fertilised eggs hatch out into small larvae. Some crustaceans have a series of free-living, usually planktonic, larval stages in their life history.

Barnacles

Barnacles are sedentary and their entire body is enclosed within protecti... calcareous plates so that they look significantly more like a mollusc than a crustacean (**page 65, above**). Barnacles may attach themselves directly onto the substrate as do the acorn barnacles, or by a stalk as is the case with the goose barnacles which are creatures of the open oceans but are often washe... ashore on logs or other floating objects. Like most sessile (sedentary) animal... they are filter-feeders. Feathery-like tentacles called cirri protrude from the confines of the barnacle "shell" to catch microscopic plants and animals tha... float past suspended in the water.

Mantis shrimps

A most ferocious reef predator is the mantis-shrimp, such as *Odontodactylus scyllarus* (**below**), so named because the large pair of claws they hold folded beneath the fore-body makes them look somewhat like a praying mantis. Mantis shrimps live within burrows, sponges or dead coral cavities. They are long slender animals with a carapace that covers the head and part of the thorax. The eyes are borne on stalks and on the second pair of antennae are large conspicuous scales which act as a rudder (see photograph) when the animal is swimming. The broad abdomen and large tail fin enable the mantis shrimp to move at very fast speeds through the water. Mantis shrimps are, very much like praying mantids, patient and stationary hunters. When suitable prey such as worms, crabs, molluscs or fish, passes their way the claws are rapidly thrust forward in a jack-knife action to catch, clutch, or spear the victim. Brightly coloured eyespots on th... inner surface of the claws not only function as species recognition marks b... may also be suddenly flashed out at an aggressor to warn or frighten it off.

Shrimps

Shrimps belong to the largest group of crustaceans called decapods that have ten pairs of thoracic legs. Decapods also include the lobsters and crayfish, squat lobsters, hermit crabs, mole crabs, porcelain crabs, and the true crabs. Many families of shrimps occur in reef waters but prawns are found in deeper waters. Many people want to know the difference between a prawn and shrimp. Prawns have three pairs of pincers and do not carry their eggs around after fertilisation but release them directly into the sea, whereas shrimps have two pairs of pincers and carry their eggs around for some time when they are said to be "in-berry".

Many shrimps live in association with coelenterates, sponges, bryozoans, ascidians, molluscs and echinoderms. The relationship may be commensal, in which case the tenant uses the host purely for protection, or may be symbiotic in which case both partners benefit from the association. Some of the delicate, almost transparent, species of shrimps belonging to the genus *Periclimenes* are free-living but many are commensal with corals, sea anemones, gorgonians, sponges, ascidians, feather-stars or sea urchins. One shrimp even lives between the spines of the Crown-of-thorns Starfish! These lovely shrimps are usually coloured and patterned to blend in with their background so that it is almost impossible for predators to detect them. The pair of beautiful little Coleman's Urchin Shrimp, *Periclimenes colemani* (**above**), named after the photographer, are almost impossible to distinguish from their sea urchin host.

A few species of snapper-shrimp of the genus *Alpheus* live symbiotically with goby fish. These shrimps, usually in a pair, excavate a deep burrow which a pair of gobies such as *Cryptocentrus cinctus* share (**left**). The fish gain shelter and protection within the shrimps' burrow and in return the fishes, by a quick movement of their tail to propel them down the burrow, warn the shrimps of impending danger. Snapper-shrimps, also called pistol-shrimps, have one exceptionally long pincer which has a peg and socket mechanism on it. When the peg is snapped down into the socket a loud cracking sound occurs which possibly frightens away predators.

Many species of shrimps such as the delicate red and white Banded Coral Shrimp, *Stenopus hispidus* (**page 32, above**), are fish-cleaners. At a chosen site, referred to by marine biologists as a cleaning-station, a pair of them wave their long antennae around to attract a fish's attention to stop and be cleaned. The shrimps nibble a fish all over to clean it of mucus, debris, fungi, and unwanted parasites. Many fish species visit these stations to be "serviced" and make no attempt to eat the cleaner-shrimps who get their own food in this way, so that the relationship is of mutual benefit to both parties.

One of the most beautiful of all shrimps to be seen on the reef is the Elegant Coral Shrimp *Hymenocera picta* (**page 32, below**). This delicate pink, white, and blue-patterned shrimp has leafy-shaped antennae and mouth parts and feeds on starfish including the Crown-of-thorns, but is not sufficiently abundant to affect numbers of this irregularly abundant starfish.

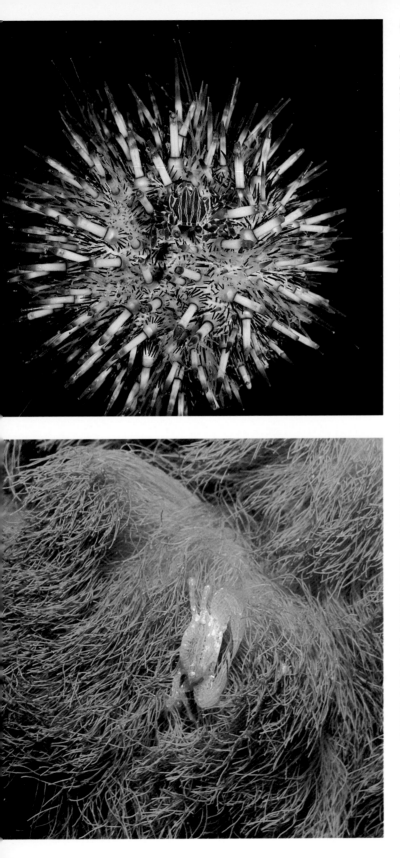

Crabs

Sponge, spanner, swimming, soldier, spider, stilt-eyed, shore, dark-fingered, pea, box, and mud crabs are just some of the crabs that can be seen on the coral reef! Most people are familiar with the stilt-eyed ghost, or sand, crabs that scamper across sandy beaches to dive down into deep burrows if pursued; or the flattened grapsid shore-crabs that scuttle over slippery rock surfaces to disappear into dark deep crevices. Swimming crabs which are easily identified by the flat "paddles" of the tips of their last pair of legs are particularly numerous on the reef and some of them such as the spiny crab *Scylla serrata* are highly edible. The first, or front, pair of a crab's ten walking legs are modified as pincers, or claws, and are well adapted to manipulate food or catch prey. Some have scissor-like edges and are used for chopping up seaweeds.

Some crabs live commensally with other reef animals and have evolved colours to match those of their host. This mimicry is clearly illustrated by the Adam's Sea Urchin Crab, *Zebrida adamsi* (**left**), which is hard to detect from the prickly background environment of its sea urchin host; and the speckled green and yellow Turtle-weed Crab, *Caphyra rotundifrons* (**below**), blends in well with the turtle-weed in which it lives. Some spider crabs, such as a species of *Xenocarcinus*, that live on sea fans are not only coloured red like their host but their body is long and thin so that it actually resembles a branch of the colony. Other crabs, instead of camouflaging themselves to look like their host in colouration, dress themselves with other reef material to make themslves cryptic. Decorator crabs apply bits of sponge, bryozoan, or debris to their carapace for camouflage and if they move to a different habitat they change their coat to suit. Sponge crabs attire themselves with a coat of sponge (see page 25).

Some of the largest and most colourful crabs on reef flats are the rock or dark-fingered crabs as they are called because they invariably have black-tips at the end of their large, well-developed, claws. Some of these crabs, such as the Shawl Crab *Atergatis floridus* (**page 34, above**), are attractively coloured and patterned. They can be found sheltering under coral or amongst rubble on reef flats, and may be herbivorous or carnivorous and feed at night or during the day.

One of the largest and most colourful hermit crabs on the reef is *Dardanus megistos* (**page 34, below**). A hermit crab's abdomen is not held under a protective hard carapace, as is the case in true crabs, but is soft and vulnerable and is spiral-shaped to fit into the whorls of a dead mollusc shell that it occupies. The back pairs of walking legs are much reduced to fit into this shell, and the first two pairs are well developed and strong for transporting the cumbersome but protective mobile home about. The visible parts of hermit crabs are usually orange or red, very hairy, and have well developed eyes on stalks. When disturbed they withdraw rapidly into the shell and block off its aperture with one claw which is usually much larger than the other. Hermit crabs are often seen lumbering over rubble and boulders on reef flats, or crawling over a sandy bottom dragging their portable home along with them.

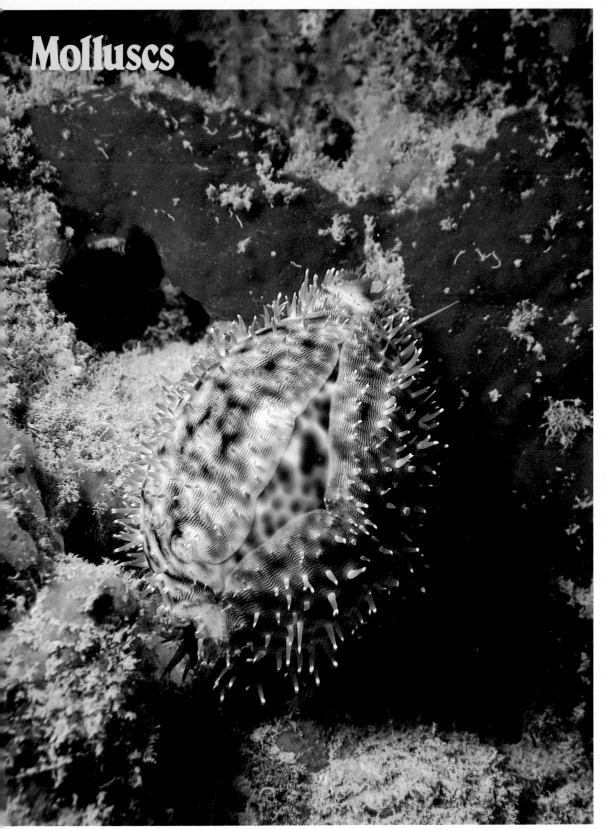

Molluscs

MOLLUSCS

There are some 100,000 species in the Phylum Mollusca and of these approximately 4000 occur in Great Barrier Reef waters. The four major classes of the phylum are the Polyplacophora (chitons), Gastropoda (univalve shells and sea slugs), Bivalvia (bivalve shells) and Cephalopoda (squid, octopus and cuttlefish), and are all well represented in reef waters. They are found on or under boulders or rubble, in crevices, amongst coral heads and algae. Some species live in the inter-tidal zone where they are subjected to exposure at low water, others favour deeper reef waters.

All molluscs have a characteristically fleshy coat, or mantle, covering the upperside of their soft body and it is this mantle that secretes the largely calcareous shell often so admired by people. In most molluscs, except nudibranchs, there is a mantle cavity between the body organs and the mantle itself which houses the the respiratory gills, or ctenidia. In some species the ends of the mantle are modified to form siphons that carry the water in and out of the body over the gills. As water passes over the gills oxygen is extracted and carbon-dioxide released. Some species are hermaphroditic and, thus, produce both sperms and eggs; whereas others have separate sexes. Clumps or strings of fertilised molluscan egg capsules attached to coral rubble and other substrates are a familiar sight on the reef. The fertilised eggs may hatch into free-swimming planktonic larva, or may develop directly into a miniature mollusc which then grows to adult size.

Univalve shells

Univalve shells belong to the largest class of all the molluscs, the gastropods. Gastropods comprise the sea and land snails that have a well developed shell consisting of one valve and the sea and land slugs that have reduced internal shells or no shell at all. The gastropod body is divided into a head that bears paired sensory tentacles and eyes that are sensitive to changes in light intensity, a muscular foot concerned with locomotion, and a visceral hump that contains all the body organs and is covered by the mantle and shell when present. The sole of the foot secretes a slimy mucus over which the snail moves by the use of cilia on the underside of the sole or by waves of muscular contractions. If danger threatens gastropods very quickly withdraw their head and foot into the shell. Attached to the foot of some species is a flat chitonous disc whilst in others it is a circular limy trap-door, or operculum, which completely seals off the shell entrance; and is a particularly useful adaptation to prevent desiccation of molluscs exposed at low tide. The limy trap doors, or cats' eyes as they are sometimes called, are often found washed up on the beach.

Gastropods may be herbivorous, carnivorous or omnivorous. They feed by using a long rasping file-like dental apparatus called a radula which can protrude from the mouth. The horny radula is covered in small recurved teeth, the shape and number of which vary from species to species. The radula is specifically adapted to scraping small bits of detritus or algae from rocks, or for catching prey such as small worms and crustaceans.

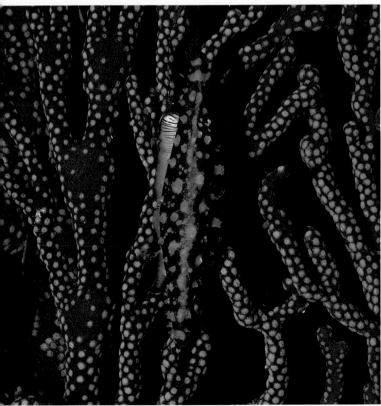

There is an immensely rich fauna of shells on the Great Barrier Reef. Whilst the classification of the shell group is based on the anatomy of the animals, the considerable variation in shell size, shape and colour has given rise to numerous descriptive common names. Top-shells, turban-shells, wheel-shells, limpets, worm-shells, screw-shells, wentletraps, periwinkles, whelks, neritids, fig-shells, tun-shells, trivias, helmet-shells, frog-shells, purples, coral-shells, dove-shells, mitres, olives, conchs, harp-shells, auger-shells, mitres, tulip-shells, vase-shells, turrid-shells and sundial-shells are some names that clearly exemplify the incredible diversity of shells !

Many shell species, such as cowries, cones, olives, strombs and murex-shells, are highly prized items for shell collections and some of them fetch much money. For centuries shells have been used as ornaments, jewellery, colour pigment and currency but it was not until maritime explorers visited the South Seas and the Great Barrier Reef during the 17th and 18th centuries that shell collecting became popular, and undoubtedly led to a notable decline in numbers of them in some areas. All live shells on the the Great Barrier Reef are now protected but whilst we protect our own shell populations the Australian authorities, sadly, permit the annual importation of countless shells to be sold to tourists who buy them under the impression they have purchased an Australian souvenir.

It is the ornately decorated cowries that are undoubtedly the most prized of all shells, and have historically been used as charms, ornaments and currency. The Money Cowry *Cypraea moneta* was once an important trading currency in the South Pacific and although it is not known when its use as money began we do know that these shells were in circulation in China during 1000 BC. One of the most distinctive features of cowries is the beauty and diversity of shell colour, texture and pattern. The shell of cowries is somewhat atypical in shape among marine gastropods, being domed and almost hemsipherical with a highly glossy outer surface. The main whorl encloses the spire and the shell aperture is long and narrow. The highly polished surface is produced by the action of the two-lobed mantle that extends out and up over the shell and in so doing protects and polishes it. The mantle often carries tubular projections and may be brightly patterned as shown in the Tiger Cowry, *Cypraea tigris* (**page 35**), the Arabic Cowry, *Cypraea arabica* (**opposite above**), and the Milk-spotted Cowry, *Cypraea vitellis* (**opposite below**). Cowries are largely tropical, shallow water, nocturnal molluscs living under boulders, amongst corals, and in crevices on the reef flat. They are mostly herbivorous, but a few may feed on sponges.

Spindle Cowries, of which several species occur on the Great Barrier Reef, are close relatives of the true cowries. They feed on soft corals and gorgonians. These lovely molluscs are usually species-specific in their feeding, which is to say they live and feed upon only one particular species of soft coral or gorgonian. Their shell is more elongated than that of true cowries and it, and the mantle, may be coloured to blend in with their host. The Toe-nail Spindle Cowry, *Calpurnus verrucosus* (**above**), lives on soft coral and the vibrant red colour of the Sea Fan Shell species of *Phenacovolva* is even more elongated to effectively hide it on its gorgonian host (**left**).

Olive shells are heavy, solid, handsome and highly polished shells that favour the sandier areas of the reef. The beautiful Red-mouthed Olive, *Oliva miniacea* (**right**), has, as it names suggest, a characteristic reddish-orange interior. The shell is cylindrical with a short spire and a notch at one end through which the mantle siphon protrudes, and the foot is large and muscular. These sand-dwelling carnivores feed mainly at night, crawling over the floor on the sole of a large muscular foot that is also used to engulf prey.

The spectacular stromb shells range in size from a few to up 30 centimetres in length. They occur on sand flats, and among coral rubble on reef flats, and are mostly herbivorous. Stromb shells do not creep on the sole of their foot like most gastropod molluscs but progress by a a series of rapid jerks. The operculum is claw-shaped and is thrust forward into the sand like an anchor until it obtains purchase and the muscular foot then contracts to draw the animal forward in a series of vigorous jerks. One of the best known strombs is the Spider Shell *Lambis lambis* (**below**), which is named for its spider-like appearance. At one end of the lip is a small notch through which one of the eyes can project.

It is quite easy to recognise the beautiful but posionous cone shells, of which there are some 70 to 80 species on the Great Barrier Reef. There is an enormous variety of colours, patterns and proportions within the general conical shape of this group. Cones are extremely predatory and actively hunt prey such as marine worms, other molluscs and small fish. Many carnivorous snails, such as cones, can "smell" their prey by means of a special chemoreceptor organ located within the mantle cavity called the osphradium. The front end of the fleshy mantle is drawn out to form a tube, called the inhalent siphon, through which water enters to bathe not only the respiratory gills but also the osphradium. This siphon projects well in front of the advancing snail and is waved around to smell out the food source, as is shown in the photograph of the Textile Cone, *Conus textilis* (**opposite above**).

The cone's proboscis bears the radula or "tongue", the teeth of which are hollow and barbed. When a cone attacks prey it actually fires one of these teeth into the prey in harpoon-like fashion. This penetrates the victim and injects it with a poisonous saliva that immobilises it. Depending on the species, this poison can be highly toxic to man. The venom of the Geographer Cone, *Conus geographus*, and the Tulip Cone, *Conus tulipa*, have proved fatal to people.

The most voracious of all reef-dwelling molluscs and one of the largest in the world is the Giant Triton, *Charonia tritonis* (**opposite below**), the shell of which may reach 50 centimetres long. All tritons are carnivorous, eating sea cucumbers and starfish. This predator is known to attack the carnivorous coral-eating Crown-of-thorns Starfish; as shown in the photograph. It was once thought that over collecting of the Giant Triton shell brought about an increase in the Crown-of-thorns Starfish numbers but this triton is nowhere abundant and it remains an open question as to whether a decline in its numbers would significantly affect starfish populations.

Volute shells have one large whorl with a short, often spiky, spire. They occur in sandy pools and lagoons and are voracious predators that feed upon other molluscs, particularly clams. They literally enshroud and suffocate prey such as a clam with the large foot and press so tightly that they force it to open its shell valves, thus providing access to its soft tissues. Volutes are very colourful and even one species such as the Heron Island Volute *Cymbiolacca pulchra*, may exhibit colour and pattern variations. These molluscs do not have planktonic larvae but instead the young hatch out directly from the fertilised egg, and settle in the vicinity of the adults so that all local populations inherit the same colour pattern. Around the coral cays of the Heron Island region there are populations with their own distinctive colour patterns. In the volute baler shell *Melo amphora* (**right**) the whorl is greatly swollen and the shell may be as long as 45 centimetres. They are commonly known as balers because they were widely used for that purpose by seafaring people.

Muricid shells such as *Murex acanthostephes* (**below**) are among some of the most beautiful shells living on the reef. They are usually highly sculptured with long or blunt spines or frilled-ridges. Bits of weed and other encrustations often get entangled among the spines and these accumulations, as well as the spines themselves, act as efficient camouflage to confuse predators. They are carnivorous molluscs that prey upon other molluscs. They feed by boring a hole through their victim's shell with secreted acid produced by glands in the foot. Their very long proboscis is then inserted through the hole and the soft flesh devoured.

The Ass's Ear Abalone, *Haliotis asinina* (**below**), is a very primitive gastropod mollusc that lives amongst dead coral rubble and crevices where it feeds on algae. Its body is covered by a large fleshy green mantle, and a large muscular foot adheres it securely to the substrate. The shell is quite flat consisting of one very much expanded whorl with a small spire, and is perforated with small holes. Water enters the mantle cavity through the gap below the shell, bathes the respiratory gills within the mantle cavity, and exits via the shell apertures. The barrier reef species is much smaller than its southern counterpart which is exploited commercially, as are many abalone species in other parts of the world. In historical times the Ass's Ear was an important food for aborigines and maoris and its shell has been used in jewellery making. Early Victorians used the shell for candle-shades, and Channel Island farmers used to string them up as scare-crows!

Not all gastropod molluscs have well developed shells. In some species the shell is reduced considerably whilst in others it is absent altogether. The very small bubble shells such as *Haminoea cymbalum* (**left**) still retain a very fragile, almost transparent, shell. This green, white and yellow mottled bubble shell is approximately one centimetre long and has a matching frilly mantle. It can often be seen in the intertidal sandy areas of the reef flat where it grazes on algae. The green, and orange-spotted, mantle partially covers the shell. These delightful little shells were first discovered in Hawaii over a hundred years ago and are now known to be widespread throughout the tropical Indo-Pacific Oceans.

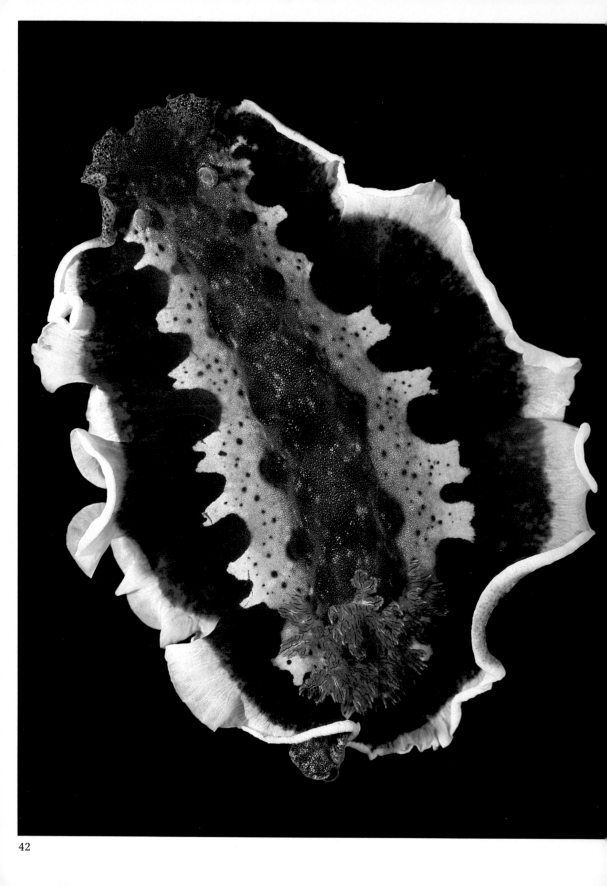

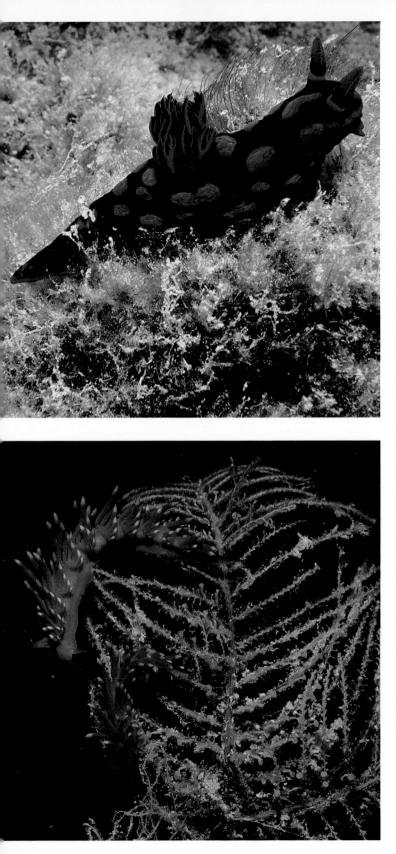

Sea slugs

Nudibranchs are gastropod molluscs that lack a shell. They are among the most spectacular and strikingly coloured animals living on the reef. The colours of nudibranchs are quite beautiful and serve either as camouflage or as a warning to predators that they are distasteful because of a poisonous fluid secreted by glands in the skin. Misappropriately named sea-slugs, these nudibranchs are ornately multi-coloured in brilliant red, pink, purple, orange, yellow, green, blue or white and occur in a number of micro-habitats from the intertidal zone down into deeper waters.

There are two major groups of nudibranchs living on the reef called the dorids and aeolids and each of these is further divided into families, the members of which have their own distinctive colour patterns. Dorids such as the beautiful Spanish Dancer, *Hexabranchus sanguineus* (**opposite**), and the Green-spotted Nudibranch, *Nembrotha kubaryana* (**left**), have a circlet of respiratory feathery gills on the back near the posterior end of the body; and on the head there is a pair of retractile tentacles and eyes. The Spanish Dancer feeds and lives upon sponges and / or ascidians whilst others, such as the Green-spotted Nudibranch, eat bryozoans. Many dorid nudibranchs are specialist feeders that have a diet limited to one, or a few, prey. Some dorids even hunt down other nudibranchs. Sponge-grazing dorids have a broad tongue, or radula, with numerous hook-shaped rasping teeth for scraping off soft tissues, whereas others that feed on ascidians may merely suck up the juices. The Green-spotted Nudibranch crawls over the substrate in the typical gastropod fashion but the large Spanish Dancer, or Magic Carpet Nudibranch as it is sometimes called, has extensive skirt-like edges to its mantle which enables it to swim through the water. The Spanish Dancer grows up to a length of 15 centimetres. When seeing this brilliant orange-red nudibranch undulating gracefully through the water it is easy to understand how it acquired its common name.

Aeolid nudibranchs, such as the Red-lined Nudibranch *Flabellina rubrolineata* (**left**), are very brightly coloured, and this colouration usually acts as warning to predators to leave well alone. This is because they have an unusual and unique way of protecting themselves that has evolved from their method of feeding. On their backs are tubular, often branched, processes called cerata that contain branches of the gut and which are concerned with respiration but which have another very important function. Aeolids feed on corals, sea anemones, soft corals and hydroids, all of which are coelenterates that possess stinging cells for their own defence and for capturing food. The aeolids extract the stinging cells from their coelenterate prey and store them in small sacs at the tips of the cerata. When aeolids are attacked by predators they fire off their stolen weapons through small pores at the tips of the cerata! This is a very remarkable example of the use of an offensive weapon of one animal by another. Aeolids also steal the symbiotic zoothanthellae from their coelenterate prey and just as coelenterates use these algae to produce food for them, so do the aeolids.

The sea slug, *Cyerce nigricans* (**below**), lives amongst and feeds upon juices of a green alga called Turtle Weed, *Chlorodesmis fastigiata*. The teeth on the radula of this vegetarian efficiently cut open the algal filaments allowing the animal's muscular pharynx to suck up the juices. The leafy extensions on the animals back contain branches of the gut as well as glands that secrete noxious substances that make the slug unpalatable to predators. It is considered that the vibrant bright orange and black colours are a warning to would-be predators of the animal's distastefulness. These sea slugs belong to a group of gastropods called saccoglossans, or sap-sucking sea slugs, and are unrelated to the true sea slugs called nudibranchs.

Chitons

Chitons or coat-of-mail shells belong to an ancient group of molluscs called polyplacophorans. Chitons have eight shell valves, and not one like gastropods or two like bivalves. These shell valves are articulated together so that, when disturbed, the chiton can roll up into a ball like a wood-louse or armadillo. Such shell valves are often found amongst sand, and because of their shape have been referred to as butterfly-shells, or by the less romantic name of toenail shells! During the day chitons cling firmly to boulders or rubble in sheltered crannies or hollows but at night they move sluggishly around grazing on algae. One of the largest chitons seen on the reef is the Gem Chiton, *Acanthopleura gemmata* (**right**).

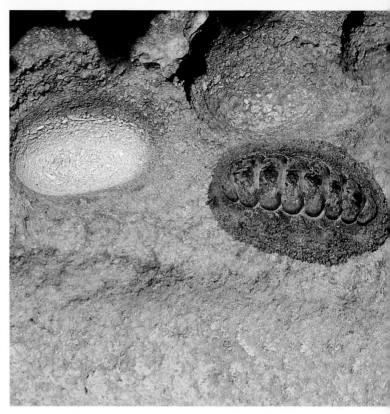

44

Bivalve shells

All bivalves have two shell valves that are hinged together with muscle and protect the two fleshy mantle lobes that enclose the respiratory gills and the body mass. Bivalves include cockles, scallops, oysters, mussels, pearl-shells, razor-shells, file-shells, clams and venus-shells. Many of them have of course long been important sea foods and oysters, for example, were cultivated by the Romans. Oyster culture in Australia began towards the end of the nineteenth century and today there are numerous farms along the coast. The large Black-lip Pearl Oyster, *Pinctada margaritifera* (**left**), and the larger Golden Lip, *Pinctada maxima*, were for many years collected for their mother-of-pearl but today only one small commercial operation remains, in the Torres Strait.

A visit to the reef would be incomplete without seeing the massive clams, that have been made so well known by stories and films suggesting they habitually snatch passing divers and drown them! They are some of the largest invertebrates on earth weighing up to 250 kilograms and reaching, perhaps, over a 100 years of age. The Giant Clam, *Tridacna gigas* (**below**), may measure one metre across and supports its massive body by its own hinge, whereas other clam species gain support from surrounding limestone rock or coral. The Giant Clam usually has its massive shell parts slightly ajar to expose its very fleshy mottled-green mantle to the light to allow millions of symbiotic zooxanthellae living there to carry out photosynthesis and produce food which the clam can then utilise, in the same way as corals do.

The Leaf Oyster, *Lopha folium* (**right**), cements itself firmly to hydroids, gorgonians, and branching corals and is itself encrusted by other organisms such as the pinkish-red sponge shown in the photograph. Bivalves such as the Leaf Oyster are filter feeders, the gills being concerned not only with respiration but also with feeding. Continual beating of hair-like cilia on the gills draw water into the mantle cavity through an inhalent siphon and oxygen and plankton are extracted from it, and waste is voided by an exhalent siphon.

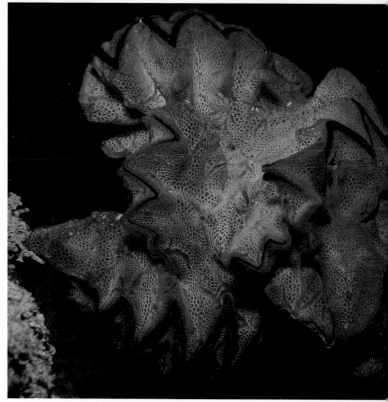

Cephalopods

Cephalopods are highly predatory molluscs that include the cuttlefishes, squids or calamaries , octopuses and the nautilus species. Some deep sea squid may be as long as 15 metres and, like the giant clams, are misleadingly depicted in many stories and films as voracious man-killers. The cephalopod head bears two prominent eyes and is surrounded by long flexible prehensile and suckered tentacles that possibly originated in evolutionary terms from the foot; hence the name cephalopod, which translates to head-foot. Octopuses have eight tentacles as opposed to the ten tentacles of cuttlefish and squid. The tentacles very effectively hold and adhere to prey such as crustaceans, molluscs or fish. The jaws or "beak" that protrude from the mouth penetrate the victim. Saliva containing a venom is produced by glands in the mouth and is injected into prey to paralyse it.

Cuttlefish such as *Sepia latimanus* (**opposite above**) have an internal calcareous shell, or cuttle-bone, that supports the somewhat flexible body. In squids this endoskeleton is little more than a horny rod, or pen, and in octopuses it is lacking altogether. Cuttlefish fill the layers of their bone with gas so that it also aids buoyancy. It is this bone that we give to our cage birds for them to obtain calcium from, and on which they may keep their beaks trim.

Squid and cuttlefish can move very rapidly by "jet-propulsion" brought about by a sudden ejection of water from the mantle cavity. Octopuses tend to be more sedentary, living in lairs in sandy substrates or within coral crevices and rubble and "creep" about in search of prey. Cephalopods have the effective escape mechanism of suddenly expelling an inky substance into the water so that they may literally disappear into their own "smoke-screen". They also have a remarkable ability to change colour very rapidly. By differentially expanding and contracting pigment cells on their skin a wave of colour moves down the body so that the animal immediately blends in with its background.

The colours of blue-ringed octopuses greatly intensify when they are disturbed. The species we illustrate is *Hapalochlaena maculosa* (**right**), the temperate water-dwelling counterpart of the almost identical but reef-dwelling species, *Hapalochlaena lunulata*. The venom of these octopuses is most poisonous to humans, as was tragically discovered recently by the death of a person handling one.

The Pearly Nautilus, *Nautilus pompilius* (**opposite below**), belongs to an ancient group of molluscs that were the evolutionary ancestors of cephalopods. This living fossil is the only living representative of the shelled cephalopods, a group that included the fossilised giant ammonites that were on earth some five hundred million years ago. It lives in deeper waters and is rarely seen, but we include it here because dead shells are sometimes found on the beach.

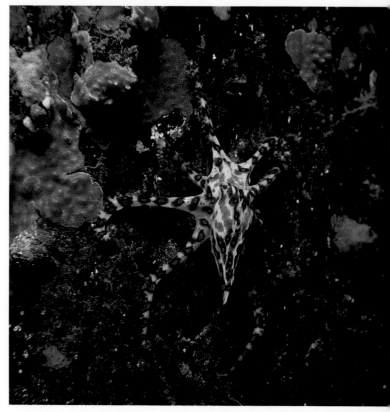

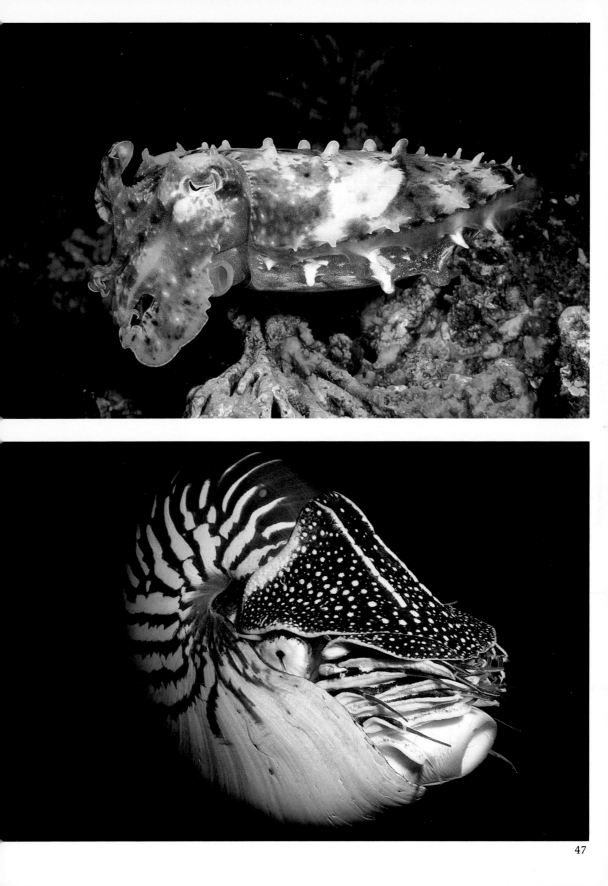

Echinoderms

ECHINODERMS

The phylum Echinodermata includes some of the most beautiful of all reef creatures and all five classes of them, the Asteroidea (starfish), Ophiuroidea (brittle-stars), Echinoidea (sea urchins), Holothuroidea (sea cucumbers) and Crinoidea (sea lilies and feather stars), occur on the reef. All echinoderms have several distinct features in common. They are radially symmetrical, which is to say that all of their body organs are repeated, usually five times, around a central disc. They have a skeleton of calcareous plates called ossicles embedded in their skin which may bear spines, and they have running through their body a complex plumbing system called a water vascular system connected to tubular extensions called tube-feet. This system opens by a small aperture called a madreporite through which water enters to keep the "pipes" saturated.

Starfish

The now infamous Crown-of-thorns Starfish, *Acanthaster planci* (**opposite**), has caused major damage to localised areas of the reef during the past few decades. This massive starfish, up to 60 centimetres in diameter, feeds voraciously on hard corals, digesting away the coral polyp flesh to leave only the dead and colourless skeletons. In 1961 plague proportions of this starfish were discovered on reefs near Cairns, and subsequently elsewhere. Scientists have suggested that population outbreaks are merely normal cyclic fluctuations in numbers and that these infestations are natural. A few animals predate the Crown-of-thorns, notably the Giant Triton mollusc (**see page 39, below**), but numbers they eat appear too small to effectively control starfish; this does urgently require research.

Starfish such as the beautiful Blue Sea Star, *Linckia laevigata* (**above**), have five arms (although some species may have more) that radiate out from a central disc and each arm contains identical sets of respiratory, digestive, locomotory, sensory and reproductive organs. The ossicles or plates, which may bear protruberances or spines, are visible and the patterns in which they are arranged varies from species to species. The Biscuit Sea Star, *Tosia queenslandensis* (**left**), has notably large skeletal plates along the edge of its arms.

On the underside of each starfish arm is a groove that houses suckered tube feet that function primarily for locomotion, but which in some species are also involved in feeding. Tube-feet can be protruded or retracted by altering the pressure of fluid within them. When tube feet contact a substrate their suckered tips adhere to the surface and by muscular contraction the starfish body is then drawn up behind them, and in this way starfish crawl about the sea floor. Most are carnivorous and feed upon sponges, corals, crustaceans, molluscs or even other starfish! By exerting immense pressure with their tube feet they can even open up bivalve shells. Starfish evert the stomach out of the mouth around their prey and secrete digestive enzymes over it to partially digest it before swallowing. On the upper surface of starfish are minute pincer-like structures called pedicellariae which pinch off any unwanted debris fron the surface to keep it clean.

The arms of the Pincushion Sea Star, *Culcita novaeguineae* (**right**), are far less apparent than in typical starfish and its granular body appears quite swollen. Starfish have remarkable powers of regeneration. Starfish are major pests on oyster farms and before their amazing regenerative powers were realised farmers would gather them up, break them up into pieces and throw these back into the sea, thus increasing the numbers of starfish rather than destroying them!

Brittle stars

Brittle stars are, as their name implies, brittle and their arms break off easily but are quickly regenerated. It is easy to tell the difference between a brittle star and a starfish. The arms of the brittle star are long and clearly differentiated from the central disc as shown by *Ophiarachnella gorgonia* (**opposite above**) and unlike those of starfish are solid and composed of scale-like ossicles joined together by muscle and bearing rows of fine spines. The tube-feet lack suckers and are not primarily concerned with locomotion but may have a sensory or respiratory function, or may aid feeding. Some brittle-stars feed on micro-organisms but most are predacious and eat small worms and crustaceans. Brittle-stars are commonly seen crawling around reef flat coral rubble by sinuous snake-like movements of their arms. Some brittle stars, such as the serpent or snake stars, have exceptionally long arms whilst others have short and branched arms as do the basket stars.

Sea urchins

Numerous sea urchin species are to be seen on the reef. Most are globular in shape but burrowing forms such as heart urchins are irregular or, in the case of sand dollars, are flattened. Most reef swimmers or divers have seen or come into contact with the black spiny Needle-spined, or Stinging, Sea Urchin *Diadema setosum* (**right**) that commonly occurs in clusters of individuals around coral boulders or amongst rubble on the reef flat, or shelters in crevices of small coral pools. The very fine spines may be as long as 60 centimetres and easily penetrate and break off in the skin. The tissue around these spines contains toxic materials that cause localised pain and swelling. Sea urchin spines vary in length, thickness, and colour and are quite mobile. The thick spines of the Slate-pencil Sea Urchin, *Heterocentrotus mammillatus* (**opposite below**), are reminiscent of implements used for writing on slates during the last century, hence the name. The spines of sea urchins obviously protect them from predation as well as assisting the suckered tubed feet with locomotion. Some of their tube-feet have a sensory or respiratory function whilst others are used for anchorage.

Sea urchins have evolved a very sophisticated masticatory apparatus called Aristotle's Lantern. This consists of 40 skeletal pieces, some of which form jaws, that protrude from the mouth and are tightly bound together by muscles and ligaments. This structure is very effective in scraping off detritus or algae from the substrate beneath the urchin.

Sea cucumbers

Sea cucumbers, or holothurians, have cylindrical sausage-shaped bodies with the mouth at one end and anus at the other. The majority of sea cucumbers seen on the reef lying amid coral rubble are usually quite drab, such as the common black sea cucumbers belonging to the genus *Holothuria*. The skin is tough and leathery with calcareous spicules embedded in it and, like that of the Prickly Red Fish Sea Cucumber *Thelenota ananas* (**right**), may have pointed protruberances all over it called papillae. Small scale worms, crustaceans and brittle stars may seek refuge between the papillae. Whilst the tough sea cucumber skin is apparently unpalatable to most predators they have nevertheless evolved a unique defence mechanism. When danger threatens they eject from their anus long sticky strands that contain a toxic substance called holuthurin. The predator becomes entwined and poisoned by these disposable threads. At a later date the sea cucumber regenerates new threads for future use. Despite the distastefulness of many holothurians some are edible and, known as bêche-de-mer or trepang, were once fished commercially in Australia.

Most sea cucumbers have tube feet along their underbody that enable them to crawl over the sandy sea floor. Around the mouth is a modified crown of feeding tube feet called the oral tentacles. These tentacles shovel up vast quantities of sand and detritus with associated bacteria and other micro-organisms into the mouth. Much of this material cannot be digested and is voided as pellets through the anus. Just as earthworms play an important role in turning over our garden soil so do sea cucumbers in turning over soft reef sediments.

Some sea cucumbers, such as the spectacularly coloured *Pseudocolochirus axiologus* (**opposite below**) are relatively sedentary and do not have locomotory tube-feet. The feeding tentacles around the mouth are, however, quite long and branched to form a network and are held upwards to trap plankton. The food is enmeshed in mucus secreted from glands in the mouth. Other sea cucumbers are worm-like ranging from a few centimetres in length to, rarely, up to five metres.

Feather stars

Feather stars and sea lilies belong to a group called crinoids that were the first echinoderms to appear in the fossil record, some 300 million years ago. These beautiful creatures are, unlike other echinoderms, sedentary and attach to the substrate either by a stalk (sea-lilies) or by small claw-like tentacles (feather-stars). Sea lilies usually occur at depths greater than 100 metres. The feather-stars (**left and below**), however, favour shallower reef waters where they can be seen attached to boulders, in crevices, or on corals on reef crests. At night these beautiful feather-stars move to a prominent position, usually where there is a good current of water, and spread out their long feathery tentacles, numbering 5 to 200 according to the species, to catch plankton. The prey is then enmeshed in mucus and passed to the mouth which, in crinoids, is on the upper surface unlike that of the starfish, brittle stars, and sea urchins. Many crab and shrimp species hide amidst feather star crowns not only gaining protection within them but also benefiting from the incoming food supply.

Fishes

ISHES

The array of spectacular reef fish swimming and foraging about colourful
ral gardens provides contrasting and changing scenes of immense beauty
posite). More species of fish dwell in this rich ecosystem than in any other
a of the oceans. They exhibit a tremendous variation in size, shape, and
our and to do justice to them would require a multi-volume set of large
resented on the coral reef.

A spectacular yet common sight to see on the reef when snorkelling is a
ed school of small coral reef fish species hovering and foraging around
lump of coral (**see page 71 & back cover**). The striking and vivid blues,
lows, and greens of angelfish, butterflyfish, surgeonfish and damselfish,
elegance of the Moorish Idol, and the delicate pink and purplish hues of
little fairy basslets illuminated by diffused rays of sunlight in shallower
ral reef waters is a sight to be remembered. The brilliant colours and
terns of many fishes have evolved specifically to enable other members of
ir species to recognise them, or to warn or deceive those of other species.
ese species-specific markings may be intensified and used during breeding
ttract a mate, or may be enlarged by inflating the body or raising the fins
warn a predator that they are distasteful or to bluff their way out of
ential danger.

Coral reef fishes of immense diversity and abundance co-exist on the reef,
iding competition through differential use of the reef's complex and vast
ources. Every conceivable microhabitat on the reef is exploited by fish
cies, be it coral rubble and boulders, coral clumps and branches, pools
l lagoons, reef flats, crests and slopes. Some fish favour more turbulent
ers whilst others seek sheltered conditions. Fish may be strictly
bivorous, carnivorous or have a mixed, or omnivorous, diet and may feed
ring the day or at night, or both. Very small fish eat plankton, slightly larger
es eat small worms and crustaceans, larger ones still eat smaller fish and
on. Some fish forage over a large area whilst others move around within
mall area referred to as a home range, or territory.

Sharks and rays

Fish can be divided into two main groups, the sharks and rays and the true
bony fish. Sharks and rays are a very ancient and primitive group of fish.
They differ from bony fish by having a skeleton of cartilage, gill slits that are
not protected by a gill cover, and by not having overlapping scales but small
granular-like plates that give a sandpapery texture to the skin instead. The
males have paired copulatory organs for the transference of sperm directly
into the female. Some species bear live young while others are egg-laying.

Sharks have streamlined bodies well adapted for fast and long-distance
swimming. Their bodies are countershaded, being dark above and pale below
thereby being hard to detect from above against the dark watery background,
and from below against the lighter surface waters. Everyone fears the
possibility of coming face to face with a shark but the vast majority of visitors
to the reef will never see one. Fortunately the predatory and dangerous Tiger
and Hammerhead Sharks favour deeper waters and rarely visit the shallows.
Four shark species occur in shallower reef waters. All are relatively small,
being less than two metres in length, and are quite harmless. One of the
commonest is the White-tipped Reef Shark, *Triaenodon obesus* (**below**),
named for its white fin markings. It is a timid and unaggressive species that
lives along the edge of reefs and over coral beds. The Black-tipped Reef Shark
is very common near reefs and coral cays, the little Epaulette Shark occurs
abundantly on reef flats, and the somewhat sluggish and delightfully named
Tassellated Wobbegong Shark may be seen in coral pools.

Electric, Manta, Eagle and Sting Rays all occur in reef waters. The giant
Manta and Eagle Rays have broad wing-shaped pectoral fins that can reach
about 5 metres in span. They may sometimes be seen flapping gracefully
through shallower waters, and occasionally will leap out of the water to fall
back into it with a great splash and noise. Smaller rays such as the Blue-
spotted Fantail Stingray *Taeniura lymna* (**page 56, above**) live exclusively on
or close to the sea floor, an existence for which they are well suited. Their
large protruding eyes lie on the upper surface of the flattened body, often half
buried into sand or sandy rubble. The small mouth is on the underside of the
body and is tightly packed with rows of plate-like teeth designed to efficiently
crush molluscs and crustaceans. The tail is narrow and whip-like and bears
two, sometimes three, venomous grooved barbed spines. If trodden on they
will inflict a most intensely painful wound. The attractive Blue-spotted
Fantail Stingray is commonly found in lagoons of barrier reef cays.

Eels

Many eels, including the morays and congers, live in barrier reef waters and may grow up to four metres in total length. Moray eels such as the *Gymnothorax* shown here (**below**) lurk beneath overhangs, amongst coral heads, or in small caverns during the day, leaving the safety of their den at night to hunt prey such as fish. Moray eels are fiercely aggressive and powerful predators with a unique way of feeding. Their razor-sharp fang-like teeth lock onto the prey and the eel then knots its body and forces the knot against the prey to firmly push against it while tearing the flesh away. Eels should not be confused with the reef-dwelling sea snakes. It is easy to tell them apart as sea snakes completely lack fins, have large reptilian scales and only their tail is flattened or compressed as an aid to swimming.

Coral cod and snappers

The coral cod family includes rock-cods, coral trout and the often massive gropers. Coral cod have a very large cavernous mouth with protruding muscular lower jaw. They are active predators upon fish and other reef animals, which they hunt at night. During the day they hide in small caverns in the coral or in crevices beneath coral boulders or rubble. Occasionally they lunge from the safety of their lair to chase off a predator, or to snap up prey. Coral cod are often brown or red in colour such as the Coral Cod, *Cephalopholis miniatus* (**opposite above**), and their colour is commonly broken up by spots or blotches to create cryptic disruptive colouration.

Very large rock cod or gropers and marlin are, together with sharks and rays, the giant fishes of the reef. The Queensland Grouper may reach up to three metres in length and weigh some 300 kilograms. Whilst the enormous size of some of these fish may be frightening many of them are very gentle and some individuals have become quite familiar and tame to fisherman and tourist operators. Gropers are difficult for anglers to catch because they habitually take bait and line beneath an overhanging coral. They are, however, easy targets for spearfishermen who have in some areas depleted large numbers and some local populations. They are now included among protected species.

It is the medium sized fish weighing anything from a few to 30 or more kilograms, such as coral cod, bream, trevallies, mackerel, wrasse, hussars, sweetlip emperors and snappers, that form an important part of the commercial fishing industry. Of course all of these fish are eagerly sought by many thousands of semi-professional, part-time, and leisure anglers. The Red Emperor Snapper, *Lutjanus sebae* (**opposite below**) is not only one of the most attractive snappers but is also considered by many to be the most delicious. Young of this species are brightly striped red and white as is the illustrated individual, and were often called "government bream" because their markings resemble red arrows on prison clothes! As they mature the colour spreads to a more uniform red.

Parrotfish

A visit to the reef is much enriched by the observation of colourful parrotfish grazing over corals in their characteristic head down and tail up foraging position. The front teeth of parrotfish such as members of the genus *Scarus* (**right**) are fused to form a parrot-like beak which is well adapted for scraping algae from the bases of living or dead coral. Soft coral polyps are also eaten by these fish, and in so-doing they leave tell-tale scrape-marks on the surface coral. Invertebrates may be eaten too. At night parrotfishes secrete a "sleeping-bag" of mucus about themselves in which they sleep, protected from predators that locate their fish prey by smell.

Male members of parrotfish schools are usually a beautiful sea-green and/or blue whereas the females and young males may be a drab red or brown. Parrotfish perform remarkable sex changes. A fish that is born a male and remains so throughout his life is referred to as a primary male parrotfish. Some parrotfish may be hermaphroditic, however, in which case they posses both male and female gonads, although both do not usually function at the same time. They commence life as a female and may reproduce for a season before changing sex to a male! Fish that do this are called secondary males. This female to male sex change also occurs in wrasse, groper, fairy basslet, angelfish and some damselfish species. In other fishes such as scorpion fish, bream, snappers and some anemone fish, the opposite occurs, with males changing to females.

Wrasse

Many wrasse occur in reef waters and some are strikingly beautiful such as the Yellow-green Wrasse, *Thalassoma lutescens* (**right**). Whilst many wrasse are mainly green some, such as the rainbow wrasses, are pigmented with all colours of the spectrum. Wrasse feed on invertebrates, such as crustaceans and molluscs, and plants. Some have tusk-shaped front teeth, rather-like the beak of the parrotfish, which may be coloured blue or green, and anglers often mistakenly refer to them as parrotfish. Some wrasse species reach two metres in length whilst cleaner wrasse are only a few centimetres long.

Cleaner Wrasse such as the Blue Streak Cleaner Wrasse, *Labroides dimidiatus* (**opposite above**), establish "cleaner-stations", where they are visited by a whole host of reef fish from very large coral cod to smaller reef fish such as the beautiful Blue Angelfish shown here. The active little cleaner fish dart over the surface of their customers eating fungal growths, parasites, and dirt from the scales and gills. They not only clean around the gills and face but will swim into the gaping mouth of larger patrons that could easily devour them. They are not eaten, however, because the service provided by the cleaner is more significant to the survival of the predator than the small meal the cleaner represents. These cleaning stations appear to be quite permanent, and several cleaner fish may operate at one of them.

Cleaner wrasse live in harems containing a male with up to 16 females. Should the male die the dominant female of the harem immediately assumes his role and within days has physiologically changed into a functional male!

Angelfish

Angelfish are tropical marine fishes that are particularly common on coral reefs. They can be recognised by an enlarged backward-directed prominant spine extending from the lower part of the gill cover (**left**). Angelfish may be coloured in brilliant shades of blues, greens and yellows arranged in spots, stripes or bands, and are perhaps the most beautifully adorned of all reef fish. The face of some angelfish is coloured and patterned differently from the rest of the body so that the fish appears to be wearing a "mask".

Many angelfish species undergo very great changes in pattern and colour with age, the adults being quite unlike the young. Five species of angelfish have almost identically coloured juveniles, but all of the adults of these species are unlike their juveniles or each other. The adult Blue Angelfish, *Pomacanthus semicirculatus* (**left**), is quite different from that of young fish which are deep indigo to black with alternating narrow and wide white lines, edged with blue. The adult is yellowish anteriorly and greenish posteriorly. The sides are profusely spotted and the body, fins, tail, gill covers and spines are edged with blue. Colours become more intense during the breeding season. The chisel-like teeth of these fish are used for scraping algae or small organisms off coral and rock surfaces. The Blue Angelfish, or Semicircle Angelfish as it is sometimes called, is one of the commonest and best known of the angelfish group, being found throughout the Indo-Pacific. This fish is held in high esteem amongst Moslem fisherman because the blue markings on the tail resembles, to them, Arabic script and possibly even words of the Koran!

The magnificently coloured Blue and Gold Angelfish, *Centropyge bicolor* (**left**), is herbivorous and lives in areas of the reef with algae-covered rubble. This strikingly coloured angelfish actively defends a territory, and lives in family groups that consist of one male and a harem of several females. The male defends a territory of a few square metres, chasing off would-be competitor suitors from his territory and harem. Sometimes a "bachelor" male is tolerated within the territory but is not allowed to associate sexually with the females. If the dominant male dies the "bachelor" may take over the harem and the territory. Alternatively, one of the females may change sex and carry out a new role as the male. Mating takes place in the summer months and the male will usually mate with all the females in his harem in turn!

Many coral fish are territorial. They will rush at anyone that comes into their territory, even a diver! Usually, however, their aggression is directed at a member of their own kind because they have the same food and space requirements. The Blue and Gold Angelfish male spends much of his time patrolling the border of his territory against neighbouring families. Border battles with a neighbour are usually a matter of performing various postures rather than physically fighting off the intruder. These angelfish can obviously recognise their own family members and this recognition may be based on how the other fish reacts and moves.

Butterflyfish

Many butterflyfish live within small schools around coral. Some butterflyfish species forage and shelter within a well defined area that is called a home range. They may patrol their home range several times a day and be familiar with every nook and cranny within it. The brilliant multicoloured blue, yellow, black or white butterflyfish usually have a dark eye stripe through each eye as can be seen in the photographs of the Black-backed Butterflyfish, *Chaetodon melannotus* (**right**), and the Striped Butterflyfish, *Chaetodon trifasciatus* (**opposite above**). Some species have distinctive "false eye" spots near the tail. The dark eye-stripe conceals the real eye to a large degree and the rear false eye markings may fool predators into attacking the far more expendable tail. The small mouth at the end of a protruberant snout has comb-like teeth which are used for delicately eating filamentous algae, coral polyps, worms or crustaceans. In some species the nose is exceptionally pointed and is used to probe food from otherwise inaccessible crevices.

Moorish Idol

The Moorish Idol, *Zanclus cornutus* (**below**), and some butterflyfishes can alter their colours and patterns at night so that their brilliance is toned down, to be less obvious to nocturnal predators, while they sleep. The Moorish Idol is so named because it is held in great respect by some moslem peoples. It is widespread throughout the Indo-Pacific and bears some resemblance to butterflyfish but is in fact more closely related to surgeonfish and, like them, is essentially herbivorous. This handsome and graceful fish is small with a long pennant-like dorsal fin and a tubular snout with small teeth, and is usually seen over branching coral in shallower waters. It is one the best known, most photographed, and certainly most elegant of all coral reef fishes; and is of course a favourite with marine aquarists.

Fairy Basslets

The delicately coloured fairy basslets, or butterfly perch, are amongst some of the smallest of the reef fish and can be seen in small schools foraging on plankton. Males are usually more brightly coloured than the females, or are a different colour altogether, and have notably longer dorsal spines. The male Blotched Fairy Basslet *Anthias pleurotaenia* (**opposite below**) is a lovely pink whereas the female is a golden yellow. A school of fairy basslets consists of females, juveniles, and a few mature males. Should a male die a female will change sex to replace it in the social structure of the school. Males are very pugnacious and appear to dominate the females at all times, perhaps to prevent them changing sex to become males. During the breeding season males actively perform courtship displays with erect dorsal fins to woo their mates.

Surgeonfish

Surgeonfish are so called because they have a sharp retractile scalpel-like spine on either side of their tail-base, sometimes protected within a sheath, which can inflict severe lacerations to a predator, and to people, if mishandled. These fish do not have a toothy beak like the parrotfish, but have bristle-like teeth for grazing upon algae. They move methodically over the algal turf in schools of their own kind, or with several other species of surgeonfish or parrotfish. Some protection is gained from living in a school for many predators do not find it easy to select, and separate, one victim from a mass of individuals. One of the most vibrantly coloured surgeonfish is the Blue Tang, *Paracanthurus hepatus* (**left**).

The elegant Purple Sailfinned Tang *Zebrasoma veliferum* (**opposite**) has sail-like dorsal and anal fins, the former developing with age into a dullish purple "sail". This very striking species is about 40 centimetres in length and feeds in very shallow waters where the "sail" is often seen breaking the surface of the water. Other fish belonging to the surgeonfish family have a lump or distinct horn on their forehead and are aptly called unicorn fish.

Damselfish

Damselfish are some of the most abundant of all of the smaller coral-reef fish. There is an immense wealth and diversity of them in reef waters and they rarely exceed more than 15 centimetres in length. The damselfish family includes the lovely blue, green or yellow damselfishes, or demoiselles as they are sometimes called, such as the juvenile Multi-spotted Damselfish, *Paraglyphidodon polycanthus* (**left**). The cross-banded humbugs, sargeant-majors, and delightful orange clown anemone fish (**page 64**) also belong to this family. Schools of damselfish are commonly seen foraging on plankton around a coral head or eating algae, and will aggressively defend a territory around their coral or algae food resource. Some of them actually "farm" a small territory by removing all but the favoured algal food, so only the food plant will grow there.

Most fishes release their gametes, eggs or sperms, directly into the sea where fertilisation then takes place. Spawning is sometimes initiated by a male performing a courtship display in front of the female. Some coral reef fish such as damselfish, however, prepare a nest site among coral, algae, or within dead shells in which they lay their eggs. When the pair are ready to mate the male dances around in front of the female showing off his colouration and fins and leads her to the nest where she lays her eggs, and he immediately fertilises them. The male, sometimes aided by the female, defends, tends and keeps the nest site clean until the eggs hatch. One species of damselfish, the Grey and White Puller *Acanthochromis polyacanthus*, is one of the few coral reef fishes to exhibit parental care, by protecting the young until they are old enough to look after themselves. If danger threatens the parents immediately lead their offspring into the safe cover of a coral structure.

The relationship between beautiful sea anemones and the spectacular clown anemone fish belonging to the genus *Amphiprion* is well known. These colourfully striped fishes, such as the Clown Anemone Fish *Amphiprion percula* (**right**), are a delight to see swimming freely amongst the otherwise stinging tentacles of sea anemones (**see also page 17**). To avoid the stinging attacks of the anemone the fish acquires an immunity by gradually covering itself with a layer of mucus secreted by the anemone that stimulates the anemone not to fire off its stinging threads. If threatened the anemone fish will dive down into the safety of the lower tentacles so that predators cannot see or reach them. Perhaps in return for this protection, these delightful fish eat waste materials from the surface of the anemone and so keep it debris-free.

Clown anemone fish belong to the damselfish family and like other members of this group they show an interesting nesting behaviour. In the case of the anemone fish a pair prepare a nest site on coral rubble, close enough to the anemone to be protected by its tentacles, which they clear of algae and debris. When the female is ready to spawn the male bites the anemone's tentacles, stimulating it to withdraw them. The male then performs a courtship dance to entice the female down to the nest where she lays the eggs which he promptly fertilises before the anemone extends its tentacles again to cover and protect the eggs!

Clown anemone fish can afford to be very bright because the anemone tentacles protect them, but some of them may in fact be cryptic within the tentacles of a brightly coloured anemone. Other fish have evolved many ways of camouflaging themselves, some to avoid detection by their predators and others so that their prey do not see them until it is too late. For example many rely on drab colouration to avoid detection, sharks and rays are countershaded, soles and flounders have special pigment in their skin that enables them to rapidly change colour and pattern, whilst other fish are disruptively coloured. Some fishes employ remarkable examples of mimicry to fool predators, like the Coral Blenny which mimics the coral it rest upon (**see page 13**). Some waspfish mimic weeds and leaves, the juvenile of a filefish species resembles a blade of seaweed, and many other fish mimic the colour patterns and behaviours of posionous species such as pufferfish.

Trumpetfish

Some fish have adapted their body shape to be quite unlike the typical fish outline. The Trumpetfish or Painted Flutemouth, *Aulostomus chinensis* (**right**), is a relative of the equally strange pipefish and sea horses. At rest this fish remains motionless, often with its tail uppermost, resembling a yellow-brown stick. This "stick" rapidly becomes a live fish, however, when a shoal of smaller fish swim by, to swiftly dart forward and suck up its victim into its distended trumpet-like mouth. The Painted Flutemouth grows to about 75 centimetres long and can move equally as fast in reverse as it can forward. It also has a peculiar habit of riding along on the back of another fish, using it in order to approach prey closely and undetected.

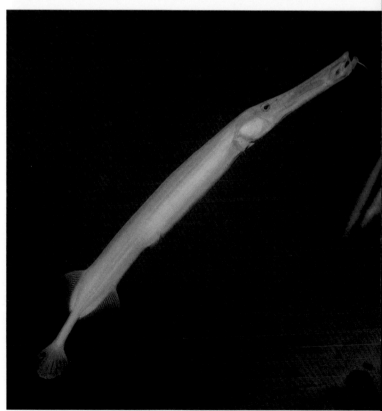

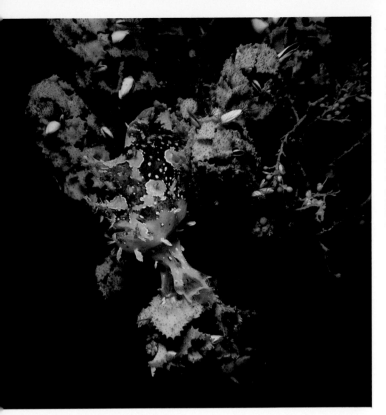

Anglerfish

Anglerfishes are masters of the art of camouflage. The yellowish Marbled or Sargassum Angler, *Histrio histrio* (**left**), is mottled and marbled with dark brown and dull orange so that it is camouflaged. Its head and body bear numerous weed-like outgrowths so that its outline is almost impossible to differentiate from the clump of *Sargassum* weed in which it lives. The dorsal fin of these somewhat bizarre fishes is extremely modified. The first spine has been displaced forward to the tip of the snout where it resembles a fishing line and lure. The lure is wiggled about to resemble a tasty marine invertebrate to attract smaller fish to it. If small fish approach the "bait" close enough the angler lunges forward with amazing rapidity and snaps up the victim into its gaping upward-pointing mouth. Note the barnacles attached to the *Sargassum* weed, that are discussed on page 30.

Stonefish and scorpionfish

Stonefish and the majority of scorpionfish are not only well camouflaged in a similar fashion to anglerfish, but possess poisonous spines that if trodden on can inflict a very severe, if not potentially fatal, wound to people. There are two species of stonefish in Queensland waters and several species of scorpionfish including the False Stonefish, *Scorpaenopsis gibbosa* (**left**). The skin of a stonefish is covered with warty protruberances, while scorpionfish have weedy outgrowths to which bits of algae and debris may adhere; all of which effectively camouflage the fish so it is almost impossible to see even at the closest range. These somewhat grotesque looking fish lie almost motionless, often partially buried, on the sea bed to await unsuspecting prey to swim past. These are quickly and efficiently sucked into their large cavernous mouths.

Stonefish have highly toxic venom sacs at the base of their thirteen dorsal spines. Some scorpionfish also have venom glands at the base of dorsal and ventral spines, whilst others have spines externally coated with venomous mucus. Venom from these spines causes excruciating pain and swelling and, in the case of stonefish, can be fatal. Medical attention should be quickly sought as there is now a very effective antivenom available that immediately counteracts the toxin. Most fatalities occur when people walk over the reef bare-footed or with inadequate footwear.

Not all scorpionfish are drab and ugly. Several members of this family, including firefish and the spectacular ornate Dwarf Lionfish *Dendrochirus zebra* (**page 66, above**), are quite the opposite. The head of the Dwarf Lionfish bears tassel-like appendages, the spines of the pectoral and dorsal fins are extremely long, and the cream and brown stripes provide an outstanding example of disruptive colouration. The fine dorsal spines are venomous and even the slightest touch will cause sudden and severe pain.

Pufferfish

Pufferfish, boxfish, and triggerfish gain protection from predators by being distasteful, and many are very brightly coloured to warn potential predators of this fact. Some other fish species mimic these fish and in so doing avoid being eaten by many predators. Pufferfish produce an extremely dangerous toxic substance called tetradotoxin that is concentrated in their liver and gonads. It is a nerve poison that, if eaten, kills predator fish and humans alike. In Japan one species of pufferfish is a delicacy and is considered an aphrodisiac. Highly qualified cooks are long trained to prepare the pufferfish dish called *fugu* in such a way that the toxin is destroyed; but there are, nevertheless, several fatalities from eating it each year!

Teeth of pufferfish are fused to form a beak but unlike that of the vegetarian parrotfish this is used for crushing crabs, molluscs and sea-urchins. Pufferfish are weak swimming, slow moving, solitary fishes of fairly shallow waters and when alarmed they swallow water or air to puff themselves up like balloons to deter predators. The Starry Pufferfish, *Arothron stellatus* (**below**), is silvery in colour and is profusely speckled with black spots, but some pufferfish species sport much brighter colours.

Boxfish

Boxfish also have a beak which, like that of the parrotfish, is used for grazing upon algae. They are so named because the head and trunk of boxfishes is encased in a protective skeletal armor-plated "box". Species such as the Ornate Boxfish, *Ostracion meleagris* (**opposite above**), are often beautifully patterned and the male, as shown here, is much more so than the drab female. Juveniles may be coloured differently from the adults. They are amusing and most attractive to watch as they swim about looking like an animated carton. The tail is often tucked to one side and the small pectoral fins whirl around like the paddle-wheels of an old steamboat. Boxfish secrete a poisonous mucus from their skin which, although harmless to humans, is distasteful to predators.

Triggerfish

Triggerfish such as the Clown Triggerfish, *Balistoides conspicillum* (**opposite below**), are strikingly coloured and have acquired their common name because of a spine-locking mechanism on the back that is formed by two anterior dorsal fin spines. The first spine can be locked in an erect position by the second spine. Triggerfish feed on crustaceans, sea urchins, and may even tackle the the Crown-of-thorns Starfish by flipping it onto its back and chewing into the less spiny and softer underside. Triggerfish build a nest for their eggs. They blow water onto a soft sandy surface to create a depression and physically remove many larger objects in the way. It is the male that tends the fertilised eggs and keeps the nest clean until the eggs hatch some five to seven days later.

OTHER MARINE VERTEBRATES

The marine reptile species of sea-turtles and sea-snakes sometimes frequent reef waters but are rarely sighted by the casual visitor. Six species of sea-turtles may occur in reef waters; the Hawksbill, Green (**right**) and Loggerhead Turtles nest on coral cays of the barrier reef whereas the Flatback Turtle, a species confined to the Australian region, favours continental islands. The Leatherback Turtle rarely nests in Australian waters, whilst the Pacific Ridley is a rare visitor. The Green Turtle, *Chelonia mydas*, is predominantly vegetarian whilst other turtle species are omnivorous or carnivorous. The chances of a visitor seeing a turtle on the reef are slight, but one may be seen taking breath on the surface. Females may also be seen on beaches when nesting. Sea-snakes are very poisonous reptiles that are usually quite shy and retiring, almost never attempt to bite, and are rarely sighted on the reef.

Dugongs, dolphins and whales are warm-blooded mammals that have stream-lined bodies suited for a completely maritime existence. They rise to the surface to breathe or to bask in the sun. Dugongs are vegetarians that eat large quantities of sea grasses in shallower reef waters where they may occasionally be spotted from a boat or plane. Schools of dolphins may be seen leaping gracefully in and out of the sea, but only divers are likely to encounter whales within the deeper waters off the barrier reef. When whales come to the surface to breathe they blow water out first, and these water spouts may be seen from a boat.

Man and the Reef

In the past large numbers of turtles, dugongs and whales were exploited for tortoise-shell, food, and oil respectively. Coastal aborigines and islanders have of course utilised the reef's rich sea food resources for many thousands of years. It was with the arrival of Europeans, and more sophisticated fishing and hunting methods, that exploitation of these sea animals began to significantly reduce, and in some cases endanger, their populations. Today the majority of the Great Barrier Reef waters are used by fishermen and countless other people for numerous forms of recreation. Game fishing, spearfishing, snorkelling and scuba diving are increasingly popular pursuits. Commercial fisherman and shell and coral collectors have to be licenced, and only Islanders and Aborigines are permitted to take turtles and dugongs under permit for food (see Foreword).

The Great Barrier Reef has long been a major tourist attraction as one of the most spectacular natural phenomenon on earth, but only now is its full potential as a world-wide and world-class tourist centre being realised. Tourists can stay in first-class floating hotels on the reef, on islands or on the adjacent mainland. High-speed vessels transport them to spectacular reef areas where they can snorkel, scuba dive, or enjoy the beauty and diversity of the reef ecosystem from a glass-bottom boat, a semi-submersible submarine or an underwater observatory. Tourists should remember at all times that the reef is in fact a very delicate and fragile ecosystem and even the slightest damage can, if repeated by others, add up to devastating and long-term destruction to an underwater wilderness that has taken literally millions of years to reach its present state.

Further Reading

BENNETT, I.	The Great Barrier Reef	
1971	Landsdowne, Sydney	
COLEMAN, N.	Australian Sea Fishes North of 30°	
1981	Doublebay, Sydney	
CRIBB, A. B. & J. W.	Plant Life of the Great Barrier Reef and Adjacent Shores	
1985	University of Queensland Press, St. Lucia	
DAKIN, W. J.	Australian Seashores	
1969	Revised Edition. Angus & Robertson, Sydney	
ENDEAN, E.	Australia's Great Barrier Reef	
1982	University of Queensland Press, St. Lucia	
GRANT, E. M.	Guide to Fishes	
1982	Fifth edition. Department of Harbours & Marine, Brisbane	
MARSHALL, T. C.	Tropical Fishes of the Great Barrier Reef	
1982	Revised Edition. Angus & Robertson, Sydney	
MATHER, P. & BENNETT, I.	A Coral Reef Handbook	
(Editors) 1984	Second Edition. Australian Coral Reef Society, Brisbane	
READER'S DIGEST SERVICES	Reader's Digest Book of the Great Barrier Reef	
1984	Reader's Digest, Sydney	
SHEPPARD, C. R. C.	A Natural History of the Coral Reef	
1983	Blandford Press, Poole	
VERON, J. E. N.	Corals of Australia and the Indo-Pacific	
1986	Angus & Robertson, Sydney	

Photographic Credits

(abbreviations following page numbers are: a = above, b = below)

Roger Steene:
Front cover upper two, (i), (iii), 5a, 8a, 9, 10a & b, 11a, 12, 13b, 14, 17, 18a & b, 19b, 20a &b, 21, 23a, 24, 25a, 26a, 28, 30, 31b, 32a & b, 34a & b, 36a & b, 39a & b, 40b, 41b, 43b, 44b, 45b, 46a, 47a, 49a & b, 51a & b, 52b, 53a & b, 54, 56b, 57b, 58a, 59b, 61a, 62, 63a, 64a, 66a, 67a & b, 71, back cover.

Neville Coleman / Australasian Marine Photographic Index:
Front cover lower two, 8b, 11b, 13a,15a & b, 16a & b, 19a, 22a & b, 23b, 25b, 26b, 27a & b, 29, 31a, 33a & b, 35, 37a & b, 38a & b, 40a, 41a, 42, 43a, 44a, 45a, 46b, 47b, 48, 50a & b, 52a, 55, 56a, 57a, 58b, 59a, 60a & b, 61b, 63b, 64b, 65a & b, 66b.

Natural Images / Australasian Nature Transparencies:
(ii), 3, 4, 5b, 6a & b, 7a & b.

Ron and Valerie Taylor / Australasian Nature Transparencies:
68.

Acknowledgements

We thank the staff of the Great Barrier Reef Marine Park Authority and the Australian Institute of Marine Science, Townsville, for help and advice; particularly Alan Dartnall, Lynda De Vantier, Terry Done, Peter Doherty, David Johnson, Carol Kenchington, Kirk Anderson, Martin Riddle, Paul Sammarco and Clive Wilkinson. We thank Peter Arnold for assistance with identifications, Wendy Richards for providing species lists, and Andrée Griffin for kindly proof-reading text. We express sincere gratitude to Isobel Bennett for commenting on a draft text. We are most grateful to Richard Kenchington for encouragement, help in numerous ways, and for writing the foreword. Paul and June Tonnoir provided much appreciated initial encouragement and support. We thank the acclaimed photographers Roger Steene and Neville Coleman for supplying their fine and sensitive work. The Australasian Nature Transparencies photographic agency of Melbourne provided additional photographs as credited above.

Index